PELICAN BOOKS
Studies in Social Pathology
EDITOR: G. M. CARSTAIRS

THE STRANGE CASE OF POT

Michael Schofield took his degree in psychology at
Cambridge University and has since specialized in
social psychology. He has conducted researches for
the British Social Biology Council, the Home Office
and the University of London, and was the
Research Director of the Central Council for Health
Education. He has published many research reports
on social problems and is the author of *The Sexual
Behaviour of Young People* (also published in
Pelicans) and *Sociological Aspects of Homosexuality.*
Recently he has published a textbook on *Social
Research.* He also carried out an educational study
for the Nuffield Foundation, which resulted in a
Schools Council Working Paper entitled *Society and
the Young School Leaver.* He is a member of the
Government Advisory Committee on Drug
Dependence, and was on the committees which
prepared the controversial report on cannabis (the
Wootton report) and the important report on Police
Powers of Search and Arrest.

Michael Schofield

The Strange Case
of Pot

Penguin Books

Penguin Books Ltd, Harmondsworth,
Middlesex, England
Penguin Books Inc., 7110 Ambassador Road,
Baltimore, Maryland 21207, U.S.A.
Penguin Books Australia Ltd, Ringwood,
Victoria, Australia

First published 1971
Reprinted 1971
Copyright © Michael Schofield, 1971

Made and printed in Great Britain by
Cox & Wyman Ltd,
London, Reading and Fakenham
Set in Monotype Times

Contents

Editorial Foreword

The author of this book is a sociologist whose name came into prominence in 1965, when he published his report *The Sexual Behaviour of Young People*, which was the product of a rigorously scientific survey of representative samples of teenagers from six localities in England. His principal research interest has been in two areas, the educational and extra-school experiences of young people and the study of various forms of social deviance. During recent years, as member of a Government committee on cannabis, he discovered that committees of this kind, if they achieve nothing else, certainly ensure that their members learn a great deal about the subject under review.

He also discovered, in a somewhat painful manner, that when an emotionally charged topic is discussed in public, the response of the popular press, of Members of Parliament, and even of the Minister concerned, can be violent and irrational rather than level-headed. This was certainly the case when the Wootton Committee on cannabis published its report in January 1969. The outcry which greeted this report was both irrational and strikingly ill informed, and this has prompted Michael Schofield to share his store of information about cannabis, and his views on how to control its misuse, with a wider audience.

He supplies us with an abundance of little-known facts. Speaking for myself, I admit to learning many things here for the first time: for example, that the term 'pot' is derived from the Mexican-Spanish *potaguaya*; that as long ago as 1894 a massive report on the drug, running to seven volumes, was published by Queen Victoria's government of that date; and that the Mayor's Committee of New York studied every aspect of this drug for years before publishing their report in 1944. Why is it that, in spite of the massive bibliography of research reports cited here, public discussions of the drug still almost invariably refer to our ignorance about its properties? Surely this is what Catholic theologians refer to as 'invincible ignorance'. The reports of 1894, of 1944 and of 1969 all had this in common, that they found cannabis to be a non-addictive drug, significantly less harmful than heroin or other 'hard' drugs, and much less often associated with violence, crime, self-injury or anti-social behaviour than is alcohol. This is something that the public, including many of their elected representatives, simply did not want to hear.

There are numerous precedents for vehement reactions against new drugs. The introduction of coffee, tea and tobacco to Europe was attended in each case with extravagant denunciations, dire warnings and even more dire penalties. It was only after their gradual adoption, in the course of several centuries, that people ceased to believe that tea undermined the character, that tobacco smoke blackened the brain, or that coffee rendered its drinkers impotent.

During the last three decades, the increased resort to psychotropic drugs has been noted with concern in countries all over the world. Partly, this is simply because they are there, in vastly increased numbers, thanks to pharmaceutical discoveries; and partly this has been a question of social learning. Hitler's *blitzkreig* of 1940 was fought by soldiers who kept fatigue at bay by taking benzedrine tablets. Since then, tranquillizers and pep pills have been taken by many of the 'norm-bearers' of the modern world, by film stars, astronauts and members of pop groups. It is easy to forget that it is not only the young who like to cloud their consciousness. As this author puts it: 'The most typical drug addict in this country is a woman of about fifty who is taking sleeping pills every night and tranquillizers every day.'

The remarkable thing about cannabis is that, unlike the new psychotropic drugs, it has been around for very many years but has only recently become a 'problem'. Long before Timothy Leary or even Aldous Huxley was born, this oriental drug attracted the interest of a group of Parisian poets and painters, who formed the 'Club des Haschischins' and experimented with its use. For generations, Indian hemp was known in Britain only as an exotic form of intoxicant patronized by Lascars and other Asiatic seafarers. It has become a matter of concern only in the post-war period, when it has been used increasingly by young people.

Today, we have the remarkable situation that members of the older generation, including many of our magistrates, know much less about cannabis than do the youngsters who are charged with breaking the law. On the whole, adult public opinion strongly condemns the use of cannabis, and this is reflected in the extremely serious penalties imposed. No less than 17 per cent of first offenders found guilty of being in possession of cannabis are sent to prison – with all that that implies for their subsequent careers. Young people accuse their elders, and the law, of confusing the dangerous 'hard drugs' with cannabis which, they claim, is less harmful than alcohol.

It seems very likely that cannabis is suspect simply because it gives pleasure. Our Protestant ethic (or what is left of it) argues that easily attainable pleasure *must* be corrupting, morally if not physically. In this debate, Michael Schofield's sympathies are very clearly on the side of the young; but he plays fair and tries to present the serious arguments, as well as the ill-informed prejudices, on the anti-cannabis side. He is well aware that where strong feelings are aroused it is easy to misrepresent the motives of one's opponents. He concedes that those who demand stern penalties against any use of pot believe that they are combating a very serious physical and moral danger – but of course the same could be said of the good people who supported the burning of witches for centuries before their fears were proved groundless. Michael Schofield does not want to 'legalize pot' until the technical problems of adulteration, standards, transition and distribution have been solved; he would prefer an interim reform of the law so that in effect the use of cannabis in private homes would not be subject to legal interference. But whatever views one holds, public attitudes and public policy where cannabis is concerned must be based on sound information, and not on prejudiced opinions, either pro or con. This book will, I believe, help all of us, young and old, to be better informed about a highly contentious topic.

G. M. CARSTAIRS

Acknowledgements

I am grateful for advice from many people who have talked to me about cannabis, some of whom are experienced users of this drug.

I should also like to thank Don Aitken, John Kaplan, Desmond Banks, and David Pedley who read the manuscript and made several useful suggestions. I owe a special debt to Anthony Skyrme for valuable comments and assistance. Bryn Ellis deserves particular thanks for his meticulous assistance during the preparation of the manuscript in its various drafts.

The publishers and I are indebted to: Bobbs-Merrill Inc. and Panther Books Ltd for permission to quote from *The Marihuana Papers* edited by David Solomon; the editor of the *Guardian* for permission to use part of an article on the use of cannabis; the editor of the *Daily Mirror* for permission to reproduce an article in an early issue; the Law Society for permission to quote from their evidence to the sub-committee on Powers of Search and Arrest.

Introduction

It seems unlikely that the problem of cannabis will conveniently disappear like teddy boys, skiffle, flower power and most of the transient fashion cults of the young. When the present younger generations have grown up, married and become parents, some of them will still smoke pot occasionally, and many others will have had this experience. Their views are unlikely to be as confused and emotional as the opinions of older adults, who can just remember their youthful flings including acts of non-conformity, rebellion, delinquency and sexual adventures, but who are in total ignorance as far as drugs are concerned. Many people are using cannabis and many more are going to use it for a long time to come, so it is only sensible to get to know more about it.

This will not be easy. It is a hornets' nest of controversy with experts coming to contradictory conclusions. Why should there be this dispute on a question which would seem, on the surface at least, not to be a hard one to answer? This is a puzzle for anyone concerned with social behaviour and this book attempts to explain the sources of this discord.

It is often said that only a little is known about cannabis, but this is not really true. Millions of words have been written about it for hundreds of years. The report of the Indian Hemp Drugs Commission in 1894 takes up seven volumes. The commission of inquiry set up by the Mayor of New York kept eminent doctors, psychiatrists, psychologists, pharmacologists, chemists, sociologists and police officers occupied for years. There have been important reports by various agencies of the United

Nations. And more recently there has been the Wootton report.

In the last few years there have been many popular books about drugs, each with a section on cannabis, and some of these have been very good (Leech, 1967; Newmark, 1968; Silberman, 1967; Drugs and Civil Liberties, 1969). I personally have read over two thousand books, articles, papers in learned journals, before starting to write this book. The problem is not the lack of information, but to sort out the contradictory observations and conflicting opinions in a mass of material that varies from quiet objectivity to emotional polemics – most of it tending towards the latter. References are given in the text and listed at the end of this book. It would have been possible, though perhaps redundant, to have cited hundreds more.

Strictly, a drug is any chemical applied to any living material to affect it in some way. A drug in the medical sense is a medicine usually prescribed by a doctor and obtained from a chemist's shop. But a drug, as the term is used in this book, is taken for comfort, stimulation or pleasure – a recreational drug. Many of these are prescribed by doctors, but a few of them, like alcohol, tobacco and caffeine, can be obtained more easily. Others, like cannabis, are illegal.

In April 1970 the Government introduced a new Misuse of Drugs Bill, but it had not completed its passage through Parliament before the General Election. As none of the main parties opposed it, a similar Bill will probably be introduced early in the life of the new Government. The new legislation proposes penalties of up to five years and an unlimited fine for possessing cannabis, and fourteen years and an unlimited fine for supplying it. This perpetuates two of the current myths about drugs: that it is the traffickers who create the demand for recreational drugs, and that severe penalties are a positive contribution to 'solving' the drugs problem. As the Assistant Commissioner of the Metropolitan Police has said: 'Some laws are passed to express public disapproval, not to be enforced.' But moral posturing is a poor substitute for informed public opinion and it has become most important that the real situation is known and faced.

The original title of this book was to have been *The Case For and*

Against Pot. It was intended to present both sides of the controversy and weigh the evidence before coming to a conclusion. But once the myths were cleared, it became obvious that the case for and against was not evenly balanced. By any ordinary standards of objectivity, it is clear that cannabis is not a very harmful drug. But the simple ranging of issues side by side is too superficial an approach for what is a very complex situation – really a social problem, much less a legal problem, and still less a medical problem.

The effects of the drug are important but there is now less dispute about the facts, particularly since the publication of the Wootton report. Obviously I have devoted several chapters to the properties of cannabis, but what is of much greater interest than the drug itself is the people who use it and the attitudes of those who do not. When you are called criminal by magistrates and police, crazy by psychiatrists, sick by other doctors, you have to be a special kind of person to go right on smoking pot. When taking cannabis arouses a strange mixture of revulsion, bigotry and fascination in the minds of the general public, there must be some basic emotional horror that brings out such an inconsistent response. As usual people are more interesting than things – even psychoactive things.

Many words are used for the drug cannabis. *Marihuana* (or *marijuana*) refers only to the leaves and not the resin of the plant,[1] but the word is used universally in America and so it occurs in some of the quotations from American books which I have used. *Hemp*, *hashish* and *hash* are other common words for cannabis. The only other word for cannabis which I have used throughout the book is *pot* (from the Mexican-Spanish *potaguaya*). This is from the vernacular, but it has now become the popular name for cannabis because it is short and convenient. Pot smokers are said to be *addicted*, *habituated* and *dependent*, but all these words apply value judgements and are best avoided. In this book cannabis is smoked, taken, used, and occasionally misused.

Whenever I talk or write about cannabis, I am asked if I smoke pot. It is an uncivil question, for a person should not be asked in public whether or not he has committed a crime. But I can see why the reader might be curious. If the writer takes cannabis, then

1. This is explained more fully in chapter 1.

obviously he has an axe to grind, and allowance must be made for his bias. If he does not take cannabis, then he cannot be fully informed about the effects of the drug. Since I was appointed to the Government Advisory Committee on Drug Dependence, several people have offered to turn me on – no doubt with the very best of intentions and to help me become better acquainted with the subject. But I have never smoked pot or taken cannabis in any form. I am sorry if this lessens the validity of my work for some readers. Incidentally, I have also written a report about child molesters, but have not assaulted any children. On balance I believe the non-user of cannabis is better equipped to write a book about pot: one does not go to a cigarette company for an impartial study of the effects of tobacco.

I have tried to be objective and I have discussed all sides of each argument as fairly as possible. But it would have been unhelpful to leave the reader to pick his way through the jungle of conflicting statements. In several cases I have expressed personal opinions after evaluating all the evidence. Therefore I must confess to one bias – fear, perhaps, is the operative word. We must avoid the sacrifice of individual privacy and personal freedom in what may turn out to be a losing battle. Consequently I have tended to favour the real instead of the ideal.

The book is divided into three major parts. In the first five chapters I present the basic information about cannabis and compare it with the other illegal drugs. In the next six chapters I try to explain the public attitudes to cannabis and discuss the main controversies. In the last five chapters I attempt to describe the legal and sociological aspects, and end by suggesting a more sensible plan of action.

1

A Description of Cannabis

In China it was called 'the Liberator of Sin'. An American described it as 'the Lullaby of Hell'. The Hindus gave it many names – usually more sympathetic, such as 'the Heavenly Guide, the Poor Man's Heaven, the Soother of Grief'. One Indian described its use as 'so grand a result, so tiny a sin'. There are hundreds of descriptions of cannabis. Max Glatt, a British representative at the World Health Organization, says that more has been written about cannabis than is known about it. In fact cannabis is a weed, a commercial product, until recently a medicine, and now a recreational drug.

Weed

Cannabis is the generic name for Indian hemp. The species *Cannabis sativa* is taken by modern botanists to include *Cannabis indica* (the form native to India) and *Cannabis americana* (the form most commonly found in the United States and Mexico). The best conditions for the growth of cannabis are high temperatures and low humidity. The plant grows for a season, dies down, then springs up again the following year from its own seed. Both male and female are necessary for reproduction. When the male plant blossoms it produces flowers that open wide, from which pollen is blown to the female plant. Cannabis is propagated only by the wind, as bees and other insects are not attracted to the plant.

The female produces seeds which are very hardy. As long as the seeds can be protected by a small covering of soil or even leaves, cannabis will spread like a wild weed. It is as hardy and spreads as easily as thistles and dandelions, or the stinging nettle which it resembles.

Cannabis grows as high as twenty feet with a hollow stalk three to four inches thick. The leaves are made up of five to eleven smaller leaflets, two to six inches in length and pointed at both ends. The upper surface of the leaflet is dark green and the underside is a lighter green with long hairs running along the bottom. When it is grown in a hot, dry climate, it has a heavy resin content which makes it sticky and gives it a distinctive odour, something like the smell of hemp rope. The flowers appear as an irregular cluster of golden-green seeds.

This bushy green plant is quite ornamental and makes a pleasant hedge if the plants are grown close together. But it is illegal to grow it in Britain or America. Laurie (1969) writes that 'it is cultivated under glass in several parts of England, notably round Windsor', but British growers have found that the resin from the local plants is not very potent. Most of the cannabis found in this country comes from the Middle East and North Africa, and the best quality comes from the Himalayan foothills of India and Pakistan; both of these countries have agreed to stop cultivation by 1986.[1]

Hemp

Under its most common name, hemp, cannabis has a long history of commercial use. For many hundreds of years it was grown all over the world, not for its resin, but for its fibre content, which is a basic substance in the production of twine, rope, bags and clothing.

Industrial users prefer cannabis grown in temperate regions where there is more rain, which makes the plants soft and fibrous and therefore of greater commercial value. The fibre content is greater when the plants are crowded together, whereas sparse planting will increase the resin content. So the best conditions for

1. Both India and Pakistan signed the Single Convention on Narcotic Drugs in 1961 which binds them to discontinue the cultivation of cannabis within twenty-five years.

commercial hemp production are quite different from those required for the copious resin which induces the maximum amount of intoxication. In temperate climates the plant is tall with strong fibres, but in hot and dry areas it is smaller and covered in a sticky golden-brown resin.

The cultivation of hemp in America was due to British initiative. The ropes needed by the British navy depended upon the supplies of hemp from the Dutch East Indies. Early in the seventeenth century this supply was curtailed, following a series of disagreements with the Dutch. To remedy this England decided to make use of its new colony in America and in 1611 the cultivation of hemp was first started in Jamestown, Virginia. By 1630, hemp had become a staple of the colonial clothing industry. But as steam power replaced sail on ships and the cotton industry was developed in Lancashire, the demand for hemp declined and by the nineteenth century its cultivation was abandoned in America.

Medicine

Cannabis has been used as a medicine throughout recorded history. It is believed that in 2737 B C the Emperor Shen Nung wrote a book which gave accurate pharmacological details about the hemp plant. For centuries hemp was the main source of clothing for the Chinese, but they also used cannabis as a medicine. Shen Nung prescribed it for 'female weakness, gout, malaria, constipation and absent-mindedness'.

In the middle of the nineteenth century various European doctors[2] noted that cannabis was used in India and Egypt to relieve pain and soothe restlessness. Before long it was welcomed as a valuable therapeutic agent. Walton (1938) reported: 'During the period from 1840–1900 there were something like over 100 articles published which recommended cannabis for one disorder or another.' Russell Reynolds (1890) wrote that 'when pure and administered carefully it is one of the most valuable medicines we possess'.

Its main use was for relieving pain, but it was also found to be

2. Particularly O'Shaughnessy (1842) and Moreau (1857).

effective in the treatment of tetanus, chorea and strychnine poisoning. It was considered useful as a remedy for headaches, migraine,
and as a sedative. It has also been recommended for easing labour
pains during childbirth and the *Journal of the American Medical
Association* reported that a baby born of a mother intoxicated with
cannabis will not become abnormal in any way.

More recently it has been suggested that cannabis may be used in
psychiatric analysis as a means of removing barriers to the subconscious. But unlike LSD, amytal, and other drugs which are
used to elicit subconscious memories and feelings which the
patient cannot otherwise communicate, cannabis tends to make
the patient more absorbed in his euphoric world and less interested
in the analysis or the psychiatrist and so less communicative.

The new synthetic analgesics have gradually replaced cannabis;
they are more effective and reliable, and are more intensely exploited by commercial firms. Cannabis preparations were used less
and less, and eventually they were removed from the British
Pharmaceutical Codex in 1954. One reason for this was the fear
that patients might become addicted, but this cannot be justified.
There is no evidence to indicate that cannabis used as a medicine
may lead on to drug abuse. In the Home Office returns on narcotic
addicts, each year there are some so-called 'therapeutic addicts'–
patients who become morphine or heroin addicts as a result of
being given the drug as a medicine. Cannabis was prescribed as a
medicine for a hundred years without producing any therapeutic
addicts.

Today there are a few doctors who are experimenting with
tincture of cannabis in the treatment of disturbed adolescents,
heroin and amphetamine dependence and even alcoholism. It is
too early to say if any of these experiments are successful. Now that
the chemical structure is being determined and synthetic variations
of cannabis are being developed (see chapter 3), it is possible that
some of these might prove to be valuable therapeutic agents.
Synthetic cannabis may have medical attributes that are as yet
unknown and, for all we know, may be quite beneficial.

Pot

Although the market for hemp is declining and the medical uses of the drug are now considered to be obsolete, as everyone knows there is a large and growing demand for the resin of this plant. The leaves, flowers and top of the plant are covered with this sticky resin which is the source of the substance which can affect the normal working of the mind and which is most often called pot, although it is said to have more than 350 nicknames.

Most of these names are simply synonyms for cannabis and they include: Indian hemp, hashish, marihuana (marijuana), bhang, ganga, charas. Cannabis is known among its users as pot, hash, grass, tea, weed, charge, etc., and is smoked in cigarettes known by users as joints, and by non-users and the press as reefers.

The ever-changing vernacular of the drug scene holds a strange fascination for some investigators. One of the very first acts of the newly formed Institute for the Study of Drug Dependence was to make a long list of all the words in the vernacular. It is not known how they intend to make use of this list when it is complete. In *Social Problems of Drug Abuse* (1968), ten of the hundred pages are used to list medical, trade and slang terms in drug lore and literature. Those listed for cannabis include: boo, sausage, dagga, herb, jingo, kif (kief), rope, shit, stick.

Keeping up with the underground vocabulary is of limited value, but the Indians have made a useful distinction in the three words they use. *Bhang* is a smoking mixture derived from the cut tops of uncultivated female hemp plants. The resin content is usually low. *Ganja* is harvested from a specially cultivated grade of the female plant. The tops are used for making a stronger smoking mixture. *Charas* comes from the same specially grown plants and consists of pure resin extracted from the tops. In England the extracted resin is usually known as *hashish*; it is made into small blocks, looks rather like an Oxo cube and is used crumbled into cigarettes. *Marihuana* is a Mexican–Spanish word, derived perhaps from the word *mariguana* (intoxicant), or perhaps from *Maria y Juana* (Mary and Jane). It was first used by the Mexicans for a poor grade of tobacco. Americans use this term when they refer to cannabis, and it usually indicates a preparation made from the flowering tops, similar to bhang. Most of these words are used in this country, but pot is the word most readily accepted and understood by everyone.

Every sort of cannabis can be obtained quite easily in Britain. Although a certain amount is smuggled into the country by well-organized criminal gangs, most of it comes into the country in small amounts, either carried by persons returning from holidays abroad or sent to immigrants by post from their home countries. Most of it is hashish, but there is a wide variety in quality and quantity, and some users complain of a glut of inferior pot each September brought in by 'amateur' smugglers.

The Confusion with Other Drugs

Almost all medicines are drugs which a doctor prescribes for us when we are ill and which we get from a chemist's shop or a drug store. But in this book it is more convenient to limit the definition to what might be called recreational drugs, and this would include alcohol, tobacco and even tea and coffee. Most people would now agree that alcohol and tobacco are both dangerous, but they are not normally included in the list when people talk about dangerous drugs.

To the general public, drug addicts are people who take heroin, reefers, pep pills and L S D. The law, the press and the public tend to think all these drugs are similar. This leads to considerable confusion and misunderstanding. There are five main groups of psychoactive drugs and it is important to discriminate between the different types. In this chapter I shall concentrate on the main medical effects, legal position and social implications of the other drugs that are so often confused with cannabis.

Amphetamines

These are stimulant drugs usually taken orally and known to the public as pep pills. Well-known amphetamines are Benzedrine, Dexedrine, Methedrine, Durophet, the once famous purple hearts, french blues and many others. Amphetamines increase energy and confidence, and induce a feeling of well-being. The really important fact about these drugs is that the user rapidly develops what is known as *tolerance* so that the pills have to be taken in ever increasing quantities to get the same effect. So there are cases when boys and girls have taken a hundred or more pills in an evening. A hundred tablets of almost anything – even sweets – would put quite a strain on the system. Connell (1958) first drew attention to the dangers of 'amphetamine psychosis', a mental condition caused by excessive use of these pills and said to be clinically similar to paranoid schizophrenia.

Possession of amphetamines is illegal except for those who have prescriptions and offenders may receive prison sentences of up to two years. There were 1,685 convictions for misuse of amphetamines in the first six months of 1969.

Although these are dangerous drugs, their use has increased year by year. Many young people take them only at week-ends to help them stay awake at all-night parties. When the idea of staying up all night loses its charm these drugs become less useful, and eventually most people stop using them altogether as they get older, marry, and settle down.

But it is not just a teenage problem. These pills are used extensively by adults, especially women, to relieve depression or fatigue, and to help them lose weight. You may remember the song by the Rolling Stones about 'mother's little helper'. In fact the amphetamines are one of the most widely used drugs in medical practice. Over the last three years there were over eight million prescriptions – about one in fifty of the total number of all National Health Service prescriptions.

In March 1970 the Government Advisory Committee on Drug Dependence produced a report on amphetamines and blamed over-prescribing by doctors for the increased use of pep pills. Most of their recommendations were incorporated into the new Misuse of Drugs Bill, and it is expected that amphetamines will be much more strictly controlled in future. Many physicians feel that the use of amphetamines can no longer be justified because there are less harmful substitutes. But a family doctor who has been prescribing amphetamines to a patient who is now dependent on them is going to have a hard time explaining why he must now stop taking them.

Although most of the amphetamines being taken are obtained

quite legally on the Health Service, there is also a black market in amphetamines which are stolen from manufacturers and chemists, and there is a certain amount of smuggling of pills made overseas. It is possible for a person to be found guilty of a drug offence for possessing pills which he bought quite legally in a foreign country.

In 1967-8 there was a marked increase in the amount of liquid methedrine, which was injected with a syringe, but supplies have now been reduced as a result of an agreement between the medical profession, the manufacturers and the Department of Health, limiting supplies of this drug to hospitals.

Cocaine is not an amphetamine but it is a powerful stimulant drug which leads to very strong psychic dependence. It is very uncommon for cocaine to be taken alone and it is most often used by heroin addicts.

Barbiturates

These are sleeping pills which can produce a dependence similar to that of alcohol. Someone who is intoxicated by barbiturates becomes drowsy and confused, unable to think clearly, or co-ordinate his muscular action, until he reaches the point of collapse – just like a drunk. His emotional control is unstable and his attitude is sometimes hostile. A person even mildly under the effects of barbiturates is a great safety hazard when driving. They are frequently used to commit suicide and there are also many accidental deaths due to taking an overdose by mistake because of the confused state of the barbiturate taker. Deaths from barbiturates by suicide have risen from 515 in 1956 to 1,490 in 1966, and deaths from these drugs by accident have risen in these years from 140 to 525 (Glatt, 1967). But there is hardly any illegal traffic in barbiturates because general practitioners prescribe it very freely and legal supplies are plentiful. Last year there were over fifteen million prescriptions for barbiturates. Barbiturates are listed as a poison and may be sold only by a registered pharmacist against prescription. It is not an offence to be in possession of this drug, nor is it included in the new Misuse of Drugs Bill, although some addicts inject barbiturates intravenously.

This is an example of a highly dangerous drug which has already become socially acceptable. It is used by the older section of the population more extensively than any drug is used by younger people. Although a large number of people use it without medical supervision, we must recognize that it helps many old people to cope with anxiety, and its control is a matter for the medical profession, not the law.

Another depressant drug which is becoming a problem is Mandrax.[1] On the drug scene a few people claim that a combination of Mandrax and alcohol can give an effect similar to LSD. But there have been many accidental deaths and suicides using this drug. The difficulty is that Mandrax poisoning looks like barbiturate poisoning, but the antidote for the latter (use of stomach pump, etc.) may be fatal if given to someone who has taken an overdose of Mandrax.

Amphetamine/barbiturate compounds (e.g. Drinamyil and many others) are very popular because they produce more euphoria and less anxiety than amphetamines taken alone, but these compounds produce many of the ill-effects of barbiturates taken on their own. Tranquillizers (e.g. Largactil, Librium) are widely used in everyday life to calm and reduce anxiety. These are not often misused. But with the possible exception of alcohol, more people are dependent on barbiturates than upon any other drug.

LSD–25

Lysergic acid diethylamide is a colourless, odourless substance which is taken orally, usually in a pill, sometimes on blotting paper or in sugar. It is a derivative of ergot, a rye fungus, and was discovered by Albert Hofmann, a Swiss chemist, who accidentally took some of this compound and experienced heightened awareness and weird distortions of colour and sound. LSD is known to pharmacologists as a hallucinogen and to users as 'acid'.

It has been used in psychiatric practice for the treatment of some types of mental illness, but only a few doctors now use this drug for

1. Mandrax is not strictly a barbiturate; it contains *methaqualone* combined with an antihistamine, *diphenhydramine hydrochloride*.

therapy in this country. In recent years it has been taken illicitly by non-conformists of all kinds including some talented writers, painters and musicians. The effect of LSD is to produce profound emotional reactions; for example, intense beauty mingled with intense horror. Timothy Leary (1964) describes the effects of LSD as ecstasy, sensual unfolding, religious experience, revelation, and contact with nature. These vivid hallucinations can precipitate severe mental disorders. There are several horror stories about people under the influence of LSD who have jumped out of windows because they think they can fly; but the number of extreme psychotic reactions may well be exaggerated.

There is considerable controversy about the ways in which LSD may damage chromosomes of living cells and even embryos in the course of development. Despite a fair amount of research and animal experiments, the evidence is not conclusive.

Unauthorized possession of LSD is now a criminal offence under the 1964 Act, and the new legislation proposes an increase of the maximum penalty from two to seven years. This drug is relatively easy to synthesize, but the raw material is difficult to obtain. Police raids confirm that it is manufactured illegally in this country, but users say the local product is often impure and prefer LSD smuggled in from the United States. It will be almost impossible to stop smuggling. Only very small amounts are needed for each trip; it is light and compact and easy to transport. Furthermore, new hallucinogens are being produced and distributed and some of these are more powerful than LSD. It is quite likely that the sellers of hallucinogens will always be able to keep one step ahead of the law.

The difficulty with LSD is that it produces such variable reactions. Even regular users occasionally have bad trips. It may be possible some time in the future to isolate the factors that produce these fearful reactions in particular people, and in regular users in particular circumstances. Until more is known about these severe reactions, leading in some cases to psychoses, this drug must be treated with caution.

Opiates

These drugs are derived from the opium poppy. In 1806 morphine was first extracted from opium and in 1898 heroin was made from morphine. These are the so-called hard drugs, described as junk and the users as junkies. These drugs are nearly always injected with a syringe, either intravenously into the blood stream ('main line') or subcutaneously ('skin popping').

The opiates are depressant drugs, still widely used to kill pain. Repeated use leads to psychic and physical dependence with unpleasant symptoms on withdrawal and a marked development of tolerance so that a continually increasing dosage is required to obtain the same effect. At first the effects of heroin are relaxation and a pleasant state of stupor, but to those who are dependent on the drug, the next fix merely banishes the terrors of withdrawal. At this stage the junkie no longer takes the drug for pleasure but as a necessity to avoid becoming physically ill. There is a high relapse rate after treatment and heroin is also physically dangerous because most users suffer from ill-health and some die from pneumonia, malnutrition, liver disease and infection due to dirty syringes.

The Dangerous Drugs Act of 1967 provides for the official notification to the Home Office of all users of heroin and other opiates. This Act also restricted the prescription of heroin to licensed doctors working through treatment centres attached to hospitals. So far these places have not got much beyond acting as *containment* centres and they appear to have had little success as *treatment* centres.

Since the restriction of prescription to licensed doctors, serious over-prescription has been avoided, supplies of illicit heroin have decreased and the price has increased considerably. Only a small amount of heroin is smuggled into the country, but it is possible to get powdered heroin (Chinese heroin) in some quarters. The heroin user frequently gets drawn into a junkie group until obtaining the drug and all that goes with it becomes his only interest and his way of life.

By now it will be clear that heroin is the addictive drug that you have read about, seen on TV and in the cinema. The junkie is the stereotype for all drug users. When people talk generally about drugs, the picture that immediately comes to mind is that dirty ill-kempt junkie living and sleeping rough with other junkies. But it is important to note that the actual number of heroin users is still small. Although the medical and social effects of heroin dependence are obviously very severe, there were less than 500 heroin addicts[2] known to the Home Office in 1969. The importance of heroin dependence has been exaggerated out of proportion to the actual numbers involved, and the attitude to other drugs and drug users has been distorted by this. Even people who now know that there is a vast difference between the effects of heroin and the effects of the other drugs still seem to regard the so-called soft drugs with the same fear as the hard drugs and speak as if all the young people in this country are in danger of becoming heroin addicts.

*

The last of the five main groups of drugs is, of course, cannabis. This will be considered in detail in the next two chapters when it will be possible to compare cannabis with the drugs noted in this chapter. A summary of the use, effects and illicit sources of all five groups of drugs is given on the next page.

2. In 1969 the total number of all narcotic drug addicts was 1,466, of which 499 were receiving heroin (either alone or in combination with other drugs) and 716 were receiving methadone; a further 251 (whose addiction is of therapeutic origin) were receiving morphine or pethidine.

TABLE SHOWING TYPES OF DRUGS

Drug	Examples	Extent of Use	Type of Market*	Type of Traffic	Duration of Use	Immediate Effects
Stimulants	Dexamphetamine Methylamphetamine Phenmetrazine Cocaine	Widespread	Grey and black	Sold by pedlars in cafes and clubs on an organized but non-syndicated basis	Phase only for most young people. Regular for adults	Lessen fatigue, increase energy, feeling of well-being
Barbiturates	Phenobarbitone Butobarbitone	Mainly therapeutic, middle-aged and elderly consumers	Grey	Negligible	Regular	Sleep, relaxation, pleasant drowsiness
Cannabis	Hashish Marihuana	Widespread among young people	Black	Organized at source outside the country but distribution in UK still localized on amateurish basis	Periodic and a few regular	Talkativeness, social relaxation, euphoria
Hallucinogens	LSD-25 Mescaline STP	Still limited	Black (smuggling and illegal manufacture)	Not highly organized	Periodic	Distortions of time, colour, sound, mystical euphoria
Opiates	Heroin Morphine Pethidine, etc.	As yet, very limited	Mainly grey	Mostly sold by registered addicts to friends and relatives. A small black market	Regular	Drowsy stupor release from reality

* The black market refers to illicit traffic in drugs obtained illicitly. The grey market refers to the illicit traffic in drugs obtained legally.

3   Physical and Psychological Effects

Medical Opinions

It should be easy to describe the effects of cannabis. After all it has been used for centuries and many doctors have tried to describe the results of using it. If that is not enough, I could, in theory, find a hundred or more cannabis smokers in order to observe and question them while they smoke.

In practice it is more difficult. Descriptions of the effects of the drug show a large number of discrepancies which may be attributed to the varying concentrations of the drug in different preparations. The potency varies widely depending on climate, cultivation and the way it is used. It has been noted that there are three grades prepared in India; ganja is two or three times as potent as bhang, and charas is the strongest of all. McGlothlin (1968) estimated that the marihuana available in the United States is one fifth to one eighth as intoxicating as the charas resin used in India. Usually cannabis is smoked, but at other times it is drunk or mixed with other ingredients to make fudge, cake or sweetmeats.

Another complication is the fact that it is often taken in conjunction with other drugs. Porot (1942) reports that most users in North Africa are also alcoholics. In the Middle East cannabis is often adulterated with cantharides (Spanish fly, an alleged aphrodisiac) or with datura and other poisonous substances. In India and the Far East it is sometimes mixed with opium which is used as a remedy for diarrhoea caused by tropical disease and impure food (Chopra, 1965).

If we decide to limit the description to the kind of cannabis smoked in this country, the reports are still conflicting. It would be sensible, and not too difficult, to verify these reports by setting up our own experiment. But if I arranged to study a group of people smoking cannabis, I would be committing a crime. Not only would I be aiding and abetting, but it is also an offence to 'permit' premises to be used for smoking cannabis.

It may be best to start the description of the effects with a few items of information which are not controversial. There is not much argument about the pharmacology of cannabis. The constituents of cannabis resin include cannabidiol and several tetrahydrocannabinols referred to collectively as THC. These are the active principles and their potency depends on the conditions in which the plant is grown as well as the way the cannabis is prepared for use. The rate and degree of absorption, and hence the effect, depend upon the way the drug is taken; the effects start earlier when it is smoked than when it is taken by mouth. There is little precise knowledge about the way THC acts in the human body, but the experienced smoker is quite knowledgeable about the different kinds of pot; he chooses carefully before he buys and has learnt the art of smoking so as to get the maximum effect. An average-sized cigarette will start to take effect within a few minutes and the effect will last from three to five hours.

It is now possible to manufacture a form of synthetic cannabis, known as delta[9]-tetrahydrocannabinol (synthetic THC). At present there is no large-scale manufacture of this substance, but it will not be long before the necessary technical processes are evolved. Some trials with synthetic THC have suggested that it is more potent and less poisonous than substances produced from the natural plant.

It is also agreed among all observers that tolerance does not develop. With most of the other recreational drugs the regular user finds that he has to increase the dose to obtain the same effect. In alcohol this is known as 'learning to hold your liquor'. But many smokers have used cannabis for years without needing to increase the amount they take. Indeed there are reports (Zinberg, 1969) that indicate that many smokers find that as they become more experienced they reduce the amount they take – a kind of reverse tolerance. Because the effects of the drug are felt soon after it is smoked, it is not difficult to adjust the dosage to achieve the effect the user seeks.

It is also agreed that even when cannabis is continually smoked over a long period, there are no signs of physical dependence. There are no withdrawal symptoms when the use of this drug is discontinued, so cannabis does not cause addiction in the proper sense of the word.

In 1964 the World Health Organization recommended the new terminology of 'drug dependence' in place of the terms 'addiction' and 'habituation'. The characteristics of drug dependence will vary with the drug used, thus it becomes necessary to designate the particular type of drug dependence in each case: for example, drug dependence of the morphine type, of the barbiturate type, etc. The WHO describes the characteristics of cannabis dependence as:

(a) Little tendency to increase the dose and no evidence of tolerance.

(b) Absence of physical dependence, so that there is no characteristic abstinence syndrome when the drug is discontinued.

(c) Moderate to strong psychic dependence on account of the desired subjective effects.

The mention of psychic dependence (more accurately described as psychological dependence) immediately takes us out of the area of general agreement. It is quite difficult to know what people mean when they talk about psychological dependence. Hundreds of Englishmen demand bacon and eggs for breakfast and feel they have not started the day properly without it. Is this psychological dependence? Usually the term is used in the sense that people are upset if they are deprived of something they like very much. Thus people could be described as psychologically dependent on chocolate, on sexual intercourse, on anything that gives pleasure. Clearly this is far too general to be a useful definition, but it is difficult to limit it in a meaningful way.

Most cannabis users can stop smoking pot without any difficulty (Watt, 1965), and the question that interests the user is unlikely to be, 'Can I stop?', but, 'Why should I stop?'. One is tempted to dismiss the whole concept of psychological dependence as just another way of saying that some people will go to a great deal of trouble to obtain what they want. But there is a bit more to it than that.

A few people are obsessed with the idea of getting a supply of cannabis when they run short, and everyone who uses it has to break the law. It is unlikely that anyone would break the law to get a bar of chocolate, but very many people would do so if sexual intercourse were illegal. The term psychological (or psychic) dependence is misleading unless it is defined more precisely. All that can be usefully said about cannabis is that a few users will do dangerous and silly things in order to get the cannabis they want, the majority will go to some trouble to get their supply, and a fairly large minority will merely take pot when the opportunity arises and will feel no distress without it. This makes it clear that the extent of psychological dependence depends in the main upon the personality of the user and much less on the intrinsic effects of the drug.

It is probably true that anyone who smokes pot every day over many years has developed a psychological dependence on the drug. The same might be said of those who take tea or coffee every day.[1] But in fact most users do not take cannabis regularly on a daily basis, but are more likely to have it at week-ends and on other occasions when they have time to spare without the smoke interfering with work or study. So they are much less likely to form a habit than those who smoke cigarettes or drink alcohol every day. Moreover it is well known that many young people take cannabis for a period and then give it up when they marry, or when they take on a new commitment, or when their circumstances change in other ways. Many of the students who take pot while at college stop smoking it when they come home. This suggests that if cannabis is habit-forming, it is a habit that can be broken without much difficulty.

We are still in a very controversial area when we attempt to describe what a person feels and how he will behave after he has

1. Regular users of tea or coffee are not usually deprived of their drug for a long period, so the withdrawal effects are rarely observed. But it has been shown that regular tea or coffee drinkers do feel distressed if they are unable to get their supply.

taken pot. There are still books being published which describe the
first signs of intoxication as nausea and vomiting, while I have met
people who claim to have smoked pot on several occasions without
it having any effect on them at all. If either of these statements were
true for the majority, there would be no cannabis problem, for
hardly anyone would bother to take it.

Sir Aubrey Lewis, Emeritus Professor of Psychiatry at the University of London, has made an extensive review of the international literature on cannabis, a total of 1,750 books and articles
beset with contradictory observations and opinions. Among the
physical effects reported are raised pulse rate and blood pressure,
tremor of tongue and mouth, cold extremities, rapid shallow
breathing, dyspepsia, pain in the abdomen, insomnia, palpitations
and headaches. The descriptions of the psychological effects cover
many pages of the review and include fixed ideas, emotional up-
heaval, hallucinations, depression, noisy laughter accompanied by
sadness, intense depersonalization and, inevitably, erotic desires.
The descriptions of 'cannabis psychosis' include schizophrenia,
paranoid states, manic excitement, depression and anxiety,
dementia, and practically every known variety of mental disorder.

In fact it is difficult to make sense of these confused descriptions
because few of the reports are specific about the dose and type of
cannabis. It is a bit like assuming beer and methylated spirits are
equally damaging. As cannabis is illegal in many countries and
home-produced in the others, there is no standardization in quality
and therefore no control over potency. Furthermore it is well
known that cannabis has a wide variety of effects depending on the
social setting in which it is taken and the mood of the user at the
time that he takes it.

Nearly all these reports quoted by Sir Aubrey Lewis come from
countries which are under-developed scientifically as well as
economically, and thus the standard of research and social investigation is less exact than we expect in this country. Consequently
it would be unwise to accept these results uncritically, especially as
regards the vague criteria for diagnosis, the likelihood of other
predisposing factors, the possible adulteration of the cannabis, and
a social situation not comparable to Western society.

The Opinions of Users

I have quoted only a few lines from the many pages of adverse effects collected by Sir Aubrey Lewis, but enough to show that they are so vague and contradictory that it is impossible to make sense of them. It is interesting to note that these authorities hardly mention any pleasant effects of the drug. Perhaps this is because they are difficult to describe, although some people have tried. The most famous attempt to describe the euphoric effect of cannabis came from Théophile Gautier, a member of the Club des Hachichins established in 1844 in Paris. The speciality of this club was a sweetmeat (Dawamesc) which contained hashish. Gautier describes the effect of eating this delicacy as follows:

After the somewhat convulsive gaiety of the beginning, an indefinable feeling of well-being, a boundless calm, took over.

I was in that blessed state induced by hashish which the Orientals call *al-kief*. I could no longer feel my body; the bonds of matter and spirit were severed; I moved by sheer willpower in an unresisting medium.

Thus I imagine the movement of souls in the world of fragrances to which we shall go after death. A bluish haze, an Elysian light, the reflections of an azure grotto, formed an atmosphere in the room through which I vaguely saw the tremblings of hesitant outlines; an atmosphere at once cool and warm, moist and perfumed, enveloping me like bath water in a sort of enervating sweetness. When I tried to move away, the caressing air made a thousand voluptuous waves about me; a delightful languor gripped my senses and threw me back upon the sofa, where I hung, limp as a discarded garment.

Then I understood the pleasure experienced by the spirits and angels according to their degree of perfection, when they traverse the ethers and the skies, and how eternity might occupy one in Paradise.

Another graphic description of hashish was written by the poet Charles Baudelaire who was a founder member of the Club des Hachichins:

Here then, is happiness, with all its intoxications, follies and puerilities. You can swallow it without fear – one does not die of it. Your physical organs will be in no way affected. . . . The simplest words, the most trivial ideas, assume a new and strange guise; you are actually astonished at having hitherto found them so simple. Incongruous and unforeseeable resemblances and comparisons, interminable bouts of punning on words, rough sketches for farces, continually spout from your brain. ... From time to time you laugh at yourself, at your own silliness and folly; and your companions, if you have such, laugh alike at your condition and at their own. But, since they laugh at you without malice, you laugh back at them without rancour.

Contemporary writers agree in essence with the sensations reported by Gautier and Baudelaire. Here is a quotation from a memorandum reported at a symposia organized by the Ciba Pharmaceutical Company in 1946:

Throughout the experiment I experienced a peculiar double consciousness. I was perfectly aware that my laughter, etc., was the result of having taken the drug, yet I was powerless to stop it, nor did I care to do so, for I enjoyed it as thoroughly as if it had arisen from natural causes. ... I awoke next morning after seven hours' sleep, with a ravenous appetite, which I think was probably as much due to the great expenditure of energy in laughing as to any direct effect of the drug itself. ... I should say that the immediate after-effect, the reaction from the stimulation of hashish, is not much greater, except for the drowsiness, than that following the common or beer garden variety of intoxication. My memory of what I said and did while under the hashish was complete and accurate.

Dr Sheldon Cholst[2] is a trained psychiatrist. The following quotation is a short extract from an essay written in 1965 while he was under the influence of pot.

This hashish, this drug, this chemical, this resin from female *Cannabis sativa* flowers, these leaves of marihuana, this poisoner of frustrating reality, this antidote for restlessness that is frustrated, this instant joy and relaxation, this chemical age-regression that allows us to be young

2. The quotations from Théophile Gautier (translated by Ralph J. Gladstone), Sheldon Cholst, and the anonymous subject reported by Victor Robinson at the Ciba Symposia are all taken from the American edition of *The Marihuana Papers*, edited by David Solomon and published by Bobbs-Merrill and in Britain by Panther Books. The quotation from Charles Baudelaire is from *The Drug Experience*, edited by David Ebin and published by the Orion Press in 1961.

and old at the same moment of time. Like being in two places at the
same time when one crosses the international date line in the Pacific
on the same day and experiences the unreal 'way out' sensation of being
in two places at the same time – it is just such an unreal feeling that
comes up in the hashish smoker. This smoke like from Aladdin's lamp
that contains the genie that brings all things to the wisher, this smoke
when inhaled does the same as Aladdin's lamp and brings out the
genius in the inhaler for he becomes fresh and comes fresh to thoughts
and ideas and he joys with laughter at his childhood pleasure. And if he
is with congenial friends he finds himself happy with them too.

More than one user has told me that the best description they
have seen comes from an anonymous pot smoker writing in the
Guardian (3 December 1969).

How strange – I remember thinking – it is exactly as people tell you it
will be, and yet until it has happened to you, you cannot have the faintest
idea what they mean. Just as in making love or giving birth for the first
time, you enter a new world of experience which, no matter how many
times you may have heard it described, still comes as a revelation to you
personally.

I felt utterly relaxed – rather sleepy in fact – and quite serene and
composed. I could feel the texture and weight of the settee with startling
clarity; could measure the precise curve of the cushion under my
elbows, and the exact depth to which they sank into it. The radiator
behind and to one side of me felt hotter to my left shoulder than to my
right: a measurable difference in temperature, though I had never
noticed it before. The texture of corduroy was microscopically detailed,
each ridge of the material distinct and separate.

Time crawled. The music went on and on. I tried to smoke an
ordinary cigarette but it tasted dry and boring and I soon stubbed it out.
The cat jumped on to my lap and I stroked her, enjoying the sleek,
glossy softness of her fur and the subtle curves and hollows of her body.
Obviously I was stroking beautifully, for she purred like mad.

The room was full of delicate vibrations of light, which shimmered
through the air. My mind too seemed twanging with these vibrations,
and my skin. They were palpable, rhythmic waves. . . . I had taken my
shoes off by now and the dense, opulent pile of the carpet felt even
better to the soles of my feet than had the corduroy of the settee to my
elbows – though still not as luxuriant as the cat. My senses were alight
with more complexity and beauty of feeling than I had ever assimilated

before. It was totally new and unimaginable. No words could have prepared me to expect this.

After a couple of hours (or so my watch recorded: it felt infinitely more) I went to bed and slept deeply and refreshingly, without dreaming. Next morning I woke with ease, earlier than usual, but full of energy and very clear-headed.

My description cannot convey the sensations I had when high; the word 'high' itself comes nearest, though I never felt disembodied or as though I were literally floating. I have simply set down with total honesty and as much clarity as I can bring to such a non-verbal experience, what happened and how it felt.

Dr Anthony Storr[3] described the effects of cannabis in a way most smokers in this country would accept: 'It is generally smoked in the company of others and its chief effect seems to be an enhanced appreciation of music and colour together with a feeling of relaxation and peace. A mystical experience of being at one with the universe is common, which is why the drug has been highly valued in Eastern religions.'

These accounts may help people to understand why so many enjoy taking cannabis although some find it hard to believe the more poetic descriptions. The truth is that the psychological effects are very variable, depending on the individual and the circumstances at the time the drug is taken. It is also true that one has to learn how to get the desired effects from taking cannabis and the experienced user has some control over the nature and course of the intoxication because he knows what to look for as the drug starts to work. But the man smoking pot for the first time does not appreciate the full effects and would probably give a misleading account if he were asked to describe them. It is well known that experienced users teach novices to notice the subtle effects of the drug (Becker, 1967).

Nevertheless it is odd that the medical and scientific accounts so rarely mention the pleasurable aspects of pot, for it would seem obvious to me that they are the most important effects of all. There is the feeling among doctors that as cannabis now has no medical use, it is therefore not worth risking any possible harm it may do, as

3. In the *Sunday Times*, 5 February 1967.

one might in the case of morphine which is both harmful and medically beneficial (like most other drugs in varying degrees). But the same argument could be used against hair dyes, sweets or swimming. The fact that all of these things give pleasure is a major argument in their favour. It would be possible to show that all of them in one way or another can be harmful, but it would be quite wrong to prohibit any of them, because the pleasure they give far outweighs the possibility of harm. Cannabis may, or may not, be in a similar category. The point I want to make here is that the possibility of injury is not of itself sufficient reason to prohibit a particular activity. But for some people, including some doctors, a substance that happens to bring happiness is suspect and a substance made solely for the purpose of giving pleasure is quite certainly unwelcome.

Four Types of Effects

The best way to avoid confusion and misunderstanding is to think of the effects of cannabis in four separate categories:

(1) Short-term effects after moderate use.
(2) Short-term effects after excessive use.
(3) Long-term effects after moderate use.
(4) Long-term effects after excessive use.

It is surprising how obscure most accounts have been about both time and quantity. So often when writers are describing the effects, it is unclear whether they are writing about physical and psychological effects while under the influence of the drug, or the effects hours and days later, or perhaps years later after continuous use. Much of the disagreement about the consequences of taking cannabis are caused by the lack of true knowledge of the amounts which have been consumed by the various groups of patients being studied and described. It will be necessary to carry out detailed studies in order to work out some standard of measurement so that it is possible to state the size of the dose and the potency of the various preparations of cannabis. Only then will it be possible to relate dose with response and so decide whether this is a drug which is dangerous (like many other drugs) when taken in overdosage and harmless in small doses.

Those conducting experiments in the US, in which cannabis is given to subjects under laboratory conditions, appear to be administrating doses far in excess of the amount of marihuana a smoker normally uses. The reports most often quoted to show that cannabis can cause psychotic reactions (Isbell, 1967; Hollister, 1968) are based on the administration of doses three times larger than would be taken by a man smoking pot to get relaxed and happy.

Short-term effects after moderate use. This is really a description of the high[4] obtained by the experienced smoker of cannabis who has learnt to use the drug effectively. He is likely to experience a relaxed feeling of well-being, deeper awareness, heightened sensitivity, sociability, and contentment which usually ends in a pleasant drowsiness. The physical effects are various, but trivial and unimportant. Even the dilatation of the pupils, the most commonly reported symptom and the one which policemen invariably look out for, is disputed by Zinberg (1969).[5]

It is reasonable to ask what is meant by 'moderate use' in this context. The best definition of moderate use is the amount required to produce the desired high. This is not difficult for the experienced pot smoker because the effect is almost immediate (unlike alcohol) and it is possible to limit the intake to the amount required.

Short-term effects after excessive use. Acute intoxication is rare because the feelings are unpleasant and a user is only likely to take more than he needs for euphoria if he is seeking temporary oblivion. Excessive use will produce a series of varying experiences which come in waves. From among the many reports on acute intoxica-

4. I use the vernacular 'high' instead of the scientific word 'intoxication' which gives the wrong impression. A cannabis smoker is high when he is in a euphoric state; this is quite different from the man intoxicated by alcohol which usually means drunk and incapable. The pot smoker's word for this is 'stoned'.

5. Since observers usually find cannabis smokers in dim surroundings, it is not surprising that their pupils are large.

tion the most usual hallucinations reported are perceiving parts of the body as distorted, depersonalization, spatial and temporal distortion. Although the descriptions of acute intoxication sound frightening to the non-user, it seems that these hallucinations are rarely horrible enough to put off a man from taking the drug again. Indeed they are not really hallucinations in the strict sense of the word, because the user is aware that the strange things he sees are the effects of the drug and he is not frightened by them as we all are sometimes by nightmares. Cannabis is not strong enough for those who wish to escape to a hallucinatory world for a time; they would turn to LSD.

The physical effects seem to be negligible and it is possible that there is a kind of self-protection caused by the quick reaction to the drug; the effects are so rapid that the user tempted to take large amounts of the drug feels drowsy and lazy before he can take enough to do physical damage. In any case cannabis does not seem to be very poisonous as the fatal dose in humans is unknown and there have been no deaths directly attributable to cannabis reported in this country.

Long-term effects after moderate use. This is the area where there is much heated controversy and many conflicting opinions. There are reports from India (Chopra, 1957) and Nigeria (Tella, 1967) on possible long-term effects, but these are not well documented. On the other hand Haneveld (1959) reports that easy availability of the drug in the Lebanon does not lead to mass dependence, nor do users increase their consumption if offered unlimited supplies. It is difficult to interpret the findings of studies made in the Middle East because cannabis is often adulterated with other substances, some of them poisonous. In fact it is difficult to understand why the controversy still rages as there have now been three authoritative reports, following detailed and careful sifting of the available evidence, and all three reports have come to the conclusion that no definite long-term ill-effects have been scientifically established.

The Indian Hemp Drugs Commission spent two years interviewing over 800 witnesses and in 1894 produced a report of over 3,000 pages. Among their conclusions were the following: 'There is no evidence of any weight regarding mental and moral injury from moderate use of the drugs.' (Ch. x para. 498.) 'The evidence shows the moderate use of ganja or charas not to be appreciably harmful, while in the case of moderate bhang-drinking the evidence shows the habit to be quite harmless.' (Ch. xi para. 510.)

In 1938 the Mayor of New York asked the Academy of Medicine to make a scientific study of the use of marihuana. A special team of thirty-one eminent physicians, psychiatrists, clinical psychologists, pharmacologists and sociologists reported in 1944. Their conclusions include the following: 'The evidence available justifies the conclusion that neither true addiction nor tolerance is found in marihuana users' (page 146). 'Furthermore those who have been smoking marihuana for a period of years showed no mental or physical deterioration which may be attributed to the drug' (page 218).

The Government Advisory Committee Report on Cannabis (often known as the Wootton report)[6] was appointed to review the available evidence on the pharmacological, social and legal aspects of cannabis. In 1969 they reported: 'Having reviewed all the material available to us we find ourselves in agreement with the conclusion reached by the Indian Hemp Drugs Commission appointed by the Government of India (1893–1894) and the New York Mayor's Committee on Marihuana (1944), that the long-term consumption of cannabis in *moderate* doses has no harmful effects' (para. 29).

Long-term effects after excessive use. There have been several reports, particularly from the Middle and Far East, which suggest that the chronic use of cannabis can cause mental and physical deterioration. Of course it is true that too much of almost anything will produce ill-effects and it is likely that there are certain personality-types who will be tempted to take large doses of cannabis over a long period. In some countries and in some situations this is not really surprising and it is noticeable that these reports suggest that this over-indulgence is among the very poor slum dwellers. When

6. The results of the Wootton report are discussed in greater detail in chapter 7.

one considers the utter misery and squalor in which the poor live in these Eastern countries, it is understandable that some of them choose to escape from the conditions by smoking cannabis in large quantities for most of the day.

Most of these reports come from countries where alcohol is against the local religion and is in any case too expensive for the poor who live in these crippling conditions. But the picture drawn by Bouquet (1951) in Tunisia, Benabud (1956) in Morocco and other more impressionistic observers is similar to the plight of the chronic alcoholics and meths drinkers to be found in skid rows in London and in most other large urban communities in Western countries.

When cannabis is taken to excess in such conditions, it is hard to distinguish between the basic personality difficulties of the individual who finds himself in this situation, the environmental effects of prolonged deprivation and malnutrition, and the effects of the drug.

It seems probable that people living in these unhygienic conditions will suffer from inertia, lethargy and self-neglect, punctuated on occasions with outbursts of violent behaviour and 'feelings of increased capability with consequent failure' (Eddy, 1965). Reports of psychoses are also to be expected from studies in these deprived areas, but again it is difficult to see if the cause is the chronic use of the drug, as Benabud (1956) suggests, or the wretched food and the appalling housing. It is remarkable that the rates of total psychoses from areas where the drug is widely used are not much different from the rates of psychoses in other areas and this suggests that if cannabis does produce a specific psychosis it must be very rare.

Most of these observers of the Eastern scene also cite individual psycho-pathological factors as prominent causes of excessive indulgence. 'You are a kif addict long before you smoke your first pipe' is a Moroccan saying which indicates that it is the personality of the user and not the drug itself which leads to chronic misuse.

But these same investigators show no concern about the moderate user of cannabis in Eastern countries just as we are not worried about the moderate user of alcohol in this country. The few cases of excessive use found in Europe and the United States appear to be individuals with very severe personality problems and cannabis seems to be a symptom, not a cause. There is no evidence that in Western society serious physical or mental ill-effects are directly attributable to the smoking of cannabis. Although pot has been smoked for many years in this country, we have not found any deleterious long-term effects and as Bewley (1965) writes: 'People who use it (cannabis) do not normally come to the attention of a doctor unless they have some other illness.'

4   Legal Aspects

The Development of International Controls

When I first came to study the arguments for and against the use of
pot, one of the strongest considerations to my mind was the attitudes of the World Health Organization and the United Nations
Commission on Narcotic Drugs. After all, there were still too few
international agreements in the world and I would not be happy to
see my own country abandon one of them. Furthermore, it is
reasonable to assume that an international organization brings
together the best experts on the subject and therefore their decisions
are likely to be right. But in fact the story of the development of
international controls is complicated and not without its doubtful
aspects.

It was at the International Opium Conference at the Hague in
1912 that it was first suggested that there should be regulations for
the control of Indian hemp (as cannabis was called in those days).
At the second Opium Conference in 1924 the Egyptian delegate
presented a strongly worded statement, containing many unproven
scare-stories and exaggerations about the consequences of taking
cannabis. The British and other representatives felt that not enough
was known about this drug to introduce complete prohibition
at a conference called to devise measures to control opium, but the
Egyptian delegate retorted that the only reason why these nations
delayed was because cannabis did not affect the safety of Europeans.

The British objection was overruled and controls on cannabis
were instituted for the first time. Ten years later a new international
commission decided that information on the effects of cannabis
'still leaves much to be desired' and set up a new committee to study

the whole problem again. But before it could complete the inquiry, the war broke out and the League of Nations ceased to exist. After the war the UN Commission of Narcotic Drugs decided not to appoint a special committee on cannabis. In 1954 a WHO Expert Committee advised the Commission that cannabis had no medical value, that 'its use eventually leads the smoker to turn to intravenous heroin injections' and concluded that 'cannabis constitutes a dangerous drug from every point of view, whether physical, mental, social or criminological'. Later statements by the WHO have modified considerably the strong language used in this document. Even at that time the Narcotics Commission decided that the new international agreement should have a special section (later named Schedule IV); this was to be a list of drugs which allowed signatory countries to decide whether to permit their use for medical and scientific purposes.

Britain signed the 1961 Single Convention along with sixty-four other countries. It is a strange document. The preamble refers exclusively to addictive drugs, but their own expert advisers had noted that cannabis was not addictive. The presence of cannabis in Schedule IV is to be explained by its obsolescence in medical practice rather than by its intrinsic danger.

No history of the development of the international control of cannabis would be complete without some mention of Mr Harry J. Anslinger. For several years before the US Congress passed the Marihuana Tax Act, there was a publicity campaign against cannabis by the Federal Bureau of Narcotics under Anslinger's direction and leadership. No story was too alarmist for this reformer. The marihuana user was said to be a violent criminal given to rape, homicide and mayhem. He also said that the drug led to insanity and to heroin addiction (although he had originally denied this possibility when giving evidence before the Senate Committee on Finance). Indeed Anslinger (1961) takes credit for many of the myths that still circulate about marihuana.[1]

1. 'Much of the irrational juvenile violence and killing that has written a new chapter of shame and tragedy is traceable directly to this hemp intoxication ...

'As the Marihuana situation grew worse, I knew action had to be taken to

The American law was passed on the grounds that marihuana was a drug that incited its users to commit crimes of violence and often led to madness. The Federal Bureau later boasted that it had destroyed 60,000 tons of marihuana. But Anslinger's influence as a hyperactive reformer went far beyond the boundaries of the United States. He was the American representative at many international meetings and at others he was able to exert considerable pressure on the delegates as the Commissioner of the Treasury Department's Bureau of Narcotics. It was also well known that the main financial support for these international organizations came from the United States.

Anslinger's moralist evangelism was bound to affect the representatives of other countries. Notices and warnings were regularly circulated by the Federal Bureau of Narcotics through the UN Commission and to the police forces of the world through Interpol. He arranged for special publicity to be given to the many horror stories emanating from Egypt.[2] When he retired his work was carried on by Mr Giordano, one of his most active disciples, as head of the Federal Bureau of Narcotics. This came under the US Treasury Department because it was intended to be a minor

---

get proper control legislation passed. By 1937, under my direction, the bureau launched two important steps: first, a legislative plan to seek from Congress a new law that would place Marihuana and its distribution directly under federal control. Secondly, on radio and at major forums, such as that presented annually by the New York *Herald Tribune*, I told the story of this evil weed of the fields and riverbeds and roadsides. I wrote articles for magazines; our agents gave hundreds of lectures to parents, educators, social and civic leaders. In network broadcasts I reported on the growing list of crime, including murder and rape. I described the nature of Marihuana and its close kinship to hashish. I continued to hammer at the facts.

'I believe we did a thorough job, for the public was alerted, and the laws to protect them were passed, both nationally and at the state level.' – *The Murderers* by Harry Anslinger and Fulton Oursler.

2. In 1960 the United Arab Republic stated that there were 900,000 Egyptians addicted to cannabis, but in 1964 the number given was under 100,000. A 1965 United Nation Document E/CN.7/474/Add.2 'Drug Abuse in the Middle East' commented on the information supplied by the UAR delegation: 'Earlier accounts have gone so far as to describe it as a plague or national calamity, without, however, producing precise information and references to support these judgements.'

tax office, but it soon grew into a large bureaucracy. Later it was combined with the Bureau of Drug Abuse under the Department of Justice.

These activities have not gone unnoticed. Professor Lindesmith (1965) has objected to the manipulation of various medico-legal reports by the Narcotics Bureau, and the President's Judicial Advisory Council criticized the activities of the Bureau in 1964. Maurer and Vogel (1967) complain that marihuana 'has received a disproportionate share of publicity as an inciter of violent crime'. The inclusion of cannabis into an international agreement mainly concerned with opiates and cocaine was due to the efforts of one determined man, combined with inadequate research methods in the countries where the drug was most prevalent and the ignorance of other delegates from countries where cannabis at that time was largely unknown.

Many people including Government spokesmen have assumed that the British law on cannabis cannot be altered as Britain is a party to the 1961 Single Convention. But article 46 of the Convention states that any signatory may denounce it unilaterally after six months' notice. It is also open to any country to propose amendments. Nonetheless it is an agreement accepted by most countries in the world after a great deal of discussion and hard work. The British representatives are surely quite right to be most reluctant to do anything which might weaken an agreement which controls the production and distribution of opium and other dangerous drugs.

The Dangerous Drugs Act 1965 and 1967

The 1965 Act implemented the Single Convention on Narcotic Drugs, 1961, which regulated the distribution of cannabis, cocaine, opiates and related narcotic drugs. It made importation, manufacture or cultivation of cannabis illegal and limited the distribution of these drugs to cases where they were prescribed by medical practitioners. As cannabis is rarely employed medically in this country and is virtually never prescribed, in effect all possession was illegal.

The concept of 'possession' can lead to legal ambiguities. There is some doubt if a person is guilty of the offence of possession if he doesn't know that he has the drug, which might have been dumped in his coat pocket without his knowledge or left hidden in his home by the previous occupier. There is also some doubt in law if a person can be said to possess a drug when all the police can find in the lining of his pocket are trace elements which can hardly be measured. There is also doubt if a person is in possession of a drug when he has just consumed it, especially as it is very difficult at present to detect the presence of cannabis in the body.

Section 5 made it illegal to permit the smoking of cannabis on any premises and there have been several cases where private houses have been entered and searched, and householders have been arrested and imprisoned. Anyone 'concerned in the management' of the premises was also liable. This is an 'absolute liability' which meant that the landlord or manager was still guilty, even if he was unaware that the premises were being used for smoking cannabis. In a recent case Stephanie Sweet was the tenant of a farmhouse near Oxford and sub-let it out to students, some of whom were arrested for smoking pot there. Miss Sweet had not visited the house for several weeks and had no idea what was going on. Nevertheless she was found guilty under this section of the Act and the case had to go as far as the House of Lords before this decision was reversed. Absolute offences are rare in English law, being confined mainly to offences like selling impure food or serving drinks to minors. The wording in section 5 was modelled on an old provision about opium dens and it is not certain whether the original framers of the Act intended to create another absolute offence as regards cannabis.

An infringement of any of the provisions of this Act rendered the offender liable to a fine of up to £1,000 and imprisonment for up to ten years. The penalties were originally introduced in 1920 to deal with traffic in opiates; they were increased in 1923 and remained virtually unchanged until the new legislation. The maximum sentences were the same for cannabis as for heroin and other much more dangerous drugs. It was often argued that the high penalties for possession were justified because it is difficult to catch the trafficker in the act of selling cannabis and it is usually only

possible to find him in possession of a large amount. It is sometimes stated that these high penalties are required by the international agreement, but this is not true. The Single Convention
obliges signatories to penalize possession, but it leaves it to each
individual country to decide the penalties that should be imposed.

The main provisions of the Dangerous Drugs Act, 1967 was to
restrict the prescribing of the drugs named in the 1965 Act to
doctors working in treatment centres. Lord Stonham stated on
behalf of the Government[3] that 'the bill is concerned with addiction
to hard drugs, and particularly with heroin and cocaine addiction'.
Just the same, cannabis was also included under its provisions.
Both these Acts really were dangerous pieces of drug legislation
because they confused heroin with cannabis. The first drafts of the
new drugs law again classified cannabis and heroin as if they were
equally dangerous, but following strong protests from the
Advisory Committee on Drug Dependence, they were put into
different categories.

The New Legislation

The 1965 and 1967 Dangerous Drugs Acts were concerned only
with drugs controlled under the international Single Convention
on Narcotic Drugs. Other Acts were passed to control other drugs.
The Government felt that the existing legislation was unco-ordin-
ated and inflexible. The new legislation repeals and replaces all
existing drugs laws. The emphasis of the new Misuse of Drugs Bill
is on speed, so that the Home Secretary can deal with any new
development of misuse that may arise.

The Bill gives comprehensive control of the manufacture, supply
and possession of all drugs which may be misused. These are
separated into three categories according to the Home Office's idea
of their gravity.

Class A includes heroin, opium, morphine and other narcotics. It
also covers LSD and injectable amphetamines which for the first
time come under a control as strict as heroin. The group also
includes some drugs not used in medicine, such as STP, DMT and

3. *Hansard*, House of Lords, 20 June 1967, col. 1,172.

DET, which have not been controlled before. It also covers cannabinol and THC.

Class B controls six narcotics and five stimulant drugs of the amphetamine type, such as Drinamyl (purple hearts), Benzedrine and Dexedrine. It also covers cannabis and cannabis resin.

Class C comprises nine named amphetamine-type drugs which are considered to be less dangerous.

An outstanding feature of the Bill is that for the first time in British drugs legislation it distinguishes between unlawful possession and trafficking which public opinion regards as deserving the severest punishment. Penalties on indictment for possession have been reduced from the maximum of ten years (which has not been used by the courts) to a range of sentences varying with the drug involved. Penalties for trafficking, supply or smuggling of all Class A and B drugs are raised to fourteen years and an unlimited fine. The same maximum penalty is provided for the cultivation of the cannabis plant.

For possession of a Class A drug like heroin, the maximum sentence is seven years or an unlimited fine or both; for the possession of a Class B drug, which includes cannabis, the maximum penalty is five years or an unlimited fine or both. Possession of a Class C drug gets a maximum of two years or an unlimited fine or both. On summary conviction the maximum penalties are: Class A – twelve months or £400 or both; Class B – six months or £400 or both; Class C – six months or £200 or both.

Another change from the old Act is that occupiers and persons managing premises are no longer absolutely liable for cannabis use on their premises. The onus is now on the prosecution to show that drug use was knowingly permitted. But the Bill extends the scope of the law so that occupiers and managers are now liable if they permit drug transactions. The new legislation, however, makes it possible for premises to be used for smoking cannabis for research.

The Bill preserves the existing powers of arrest and search, which were the subject of consideration by the Deedes committee. Thus the power of statutory search, which first appeared in the 1967 Act, is to be continued despite criticism of the way these police powers are being used.

The Home Secretary is also given wide powers to ban a doctor from prescribing drugs when a tribunal has decided that he has been over-prescribing. But as cannabis is hardly ever prescribed, these regulations will not affect pot smokers. The Home Secretary can also add to the list of drugs, or change the category of a particular drug from one class to another by regulations, subject to the approval of Parliament. An advisory council and a committee of experts will be set up to assist the Home Secretary. These bodies – with tribunal procedures for erring doctors – are offered as safeguards against the wide powers the Bill gives the Home Secretary.

The alteration in the maximum sentences for cannabis will have very little effect as the new penalties are higher than the courts sensibly impose. It seems that the Government has accepted that there should be some legal indication that heroin is more dangerous than cannabis, but both should be subject to heavy penalties. It remains to be seen if the change means that the police will concentrate on the dealer and show less enthusiasm for arresting the ordinary user of cannabis. With a maximum penalty of five years, possession is still far more than a technical offence.

The Number of Offenders

The total number of persons convicted under the 1965 Act in 1969 was 6,095; of these, 4,683 were convicted for cannabis offences. The total number of persons convicted for all offences under the various Drug Acts was 9,857 in 1969, so about half of all offenders were penalized for using cannabis. Most of the other offences were for possessing amphetamines. There has been a steep rise in the number of offences involving cannabis from 17 in 1946 to 205 in 1954, to 4,683 in 1969 – an increase of 52 per cent over the previous year. No doubt part of this growth is due to additional police activity, but most people would agree that there has been a tremendous increase in cannabis use in the last few years, especially among the young. Originally most of the offenders were immigrants but in recent years over half of the offenders have been of

United Kingdom origin. Of the 4,683 convictions, 4,094 were for unlawful possession, 122 for unlawful import, 147 for unlawful supply, 225 for permitting premises to be used for smoking cannabis, 49 for procuring and 46 for other offences. Five people were convicted for cultivating cannabis in England, but only a few plants were found. In 1969 the police and customs seized 544 kilogrammes of cannabis herb and resin, compared with 1,125 kilogrammes in 1968. The amount seized in the last two years would make more than 1,000,000 joints. The confiscated cannabis came from twenty-five different countries.

Over two thirds of all cannabis offenders did not have any convictions of any kind for non-drug offences. About a quarter of all cannabis offenders were imprisoned; about 17 per cent of first offenders were sent to prison (or borstal, detention centre or approved school).

A special analysis was made for the Wootton Committee, which analysed all cannabis convictions in 1967 according to the amount of the drug found on the offender. In fact nine out of ten of all offences were for possessing less than 30 grams. Of the 2,419 people who were convicted of possessing less than 30 grams of cannabis, 373 (15 per cent) were imprisoned – the Wootton committee felt that this proportion was far too high. The same analysis showed that 1,857 persons without previous convictions for any type of offence were convicted of possessing less than 30 grams of cannabis; 237 (13 per cent) of these first offenders were sent to prison – 119 of them were aged twenty-five or under.

It appears that cannabis smokers are not criminals in the usual sense of the word. In general they do not commit other crimes and most of them are young first offenders. The vast majority have less than 30 grams in their possession when they are arrested. Of the 2,419 persons convicted of possessing this small amount of cannabis in 1967, only 191 (less than 8 per cent) had previous convictions for drug offences. This may suggest that first offenders give up taking cannabis after a conviction for possessing; a more probable explanation is that the convictions only reflect a very small proportion of the total number of cannabis users and detection is mostly a matter of chance.

Illicit Sources of Supply

In 1966 a report by the Economic and Social Council of the Permanent Central Narcotics Board observed that the illegal traffic in cannabis was the most widespread of all. The quantities of cannabis seized varies widely from country to country and depends more upon the efficiency of the customs officials than the amount actually leaving or entering a country. There is no doubt that the smuggling is international with variations in the degree of organization.

In Great Britain the annual volume of seizures had not increased very much between 1957 and 1967. There have been a few cases where people were caught bringing in very large supplies, but most seizures have been of small amounts from seamen and people returning from holidays abroad. The annual report from the Home Office to the United Nations for 1965 noted 'the apparently new practice of individuals from different groups of cannabis users making visits to Asia via Europe, often by hitch-hiking, with the object of purchasing supplies for resale to United Kingdom users known to them'.

The traffic in cannabis had been for many years linked with ports and dockland districts and was destined mostly for seamen, musicians and immigrants. By 1960 the use of cannabis had spread beyond these groups and was no longer restricted to inner London. There was also a social expansion because the drug was now being used not only by musicians and artists, but by a significant section of the population. Even so, there are no signs that criminal gangs have started large-scale smuggling of cannabis although this has for a long time been a possibility. As things are at present it would not be worth the while of a bigtime crook. Supplies are plentiful and there are so many sources of supply that it would be impossible to create a monopoly. If the police were very successful and caused a scarcity, thereby putting up the black-market price, a large organized criminal group might enter the field. But at present cannabis is a business for the small operator.

Recently three men were discovered smuggling in 414 pounds of cannabis resin. They were each imprisoned for five years and fined

£2,000; in default of the fine, they will serve two more years. They were breaking the law and no doubt would have made a lot of money from selling the hashish if they had not been caught. Therefore most people would agree that they deserved to be given a heavy fine and sent to prison. Smuggling on this large scale seems to be very rare. Of the 2,731 convicted of cannabis offences in 1967, only 49 (1·8 per cent) were found guilty of possessing more than one kilogram.

The emotion and hatred engendered by the idea of an evil pusher trapping young people and tricking them into becoming drug addicts is misplaced. Many people professing a liberal attitude to young people and drugs have suggested decreasing the penalties for people who take cannabis and increasing the penalties for those who sell it. But this extravagant hatred of the pusher is based on a myth which is misleading. The very word 'pusher' is emotive and conjures up the picture of the evil man tricking innocent young people into trying a drug with the certain knowledge that once they have been trapped in this way, they will be hooked for life. This picture is not true even for heroin, and is a long way from the truth for cannabis which is not an addictive drug.

Furthermore it is not true that heroin and pot are usually obtained from the same supplier. Nearly all cannabis is smuggled into the country in small amounts. Very little heroin comes from abroad; the main source of illegal heroin comes from addicts who have managed to persuade their doctor to prescribe more than they need and they sell this to people who have not yet registered at a treatment centre. Pot smokers and junkies do not mix. The average user of cannabis does not know anyone who takes heroin and he certainly would not know where to get a supply.

The new Act awards the same penalties for selling heroin or cannabis. Thus it perpetuates two of the common myths – that the problem can be solved by attacking the dealer in drugs, and that heroin and cannabis are obtained from the same supplier.

People who buy and sell pot do not behave like the ordinary man's idea of the mythical pusher. An experienced pot smoker knows where to go for a new supply and probably has a regular dealer. Knowing that the police set traps and use *agents pro-*

vocateurs, the sensible smoker realizes that this is a dangerous transaction and will only deal with someone he can trust, or at the very least with someone who has been recommended by another user.

Pot smoking is a gregarious activity and so a person who has just begun smoking will probably be given or sold a small amount by a friend. For quite a time the user will get his supplies from others in his circle and will not have to find a supplier dealing in cannabis for profit. Eventually he may want to get his own supply and then he finds out from his friends where to go. But even if he does not get this friendly advice, he can probably find a small-time dealer by asking around.

Of course there is always a risk that a person buying an illegal substance may be swindled because the seller will know that the cheated buyer will not complain to the police. Sometimes the buyer is required to pay in advance and the seller goes away to get the hash, and disappears for ever. On other occasions the buyer finds he has been sold pot which is of a very poor quality or has been adulterated to make it go further. On more than one occasion the police have arrested someone for possessing cannabis, but on analysis it turned out to be a harmless substance such as herbal mixture although the user was even more surprised than the police to be given this information.

Quite often the sale of cannabis is a social occasion with the seller arriving at the client's home with his scales and supplies, and the buyer looking it over and talking knowledgeably about the quality and the current market rate. One of the services provided by *IT* is a periodical run down of the state of the market (see illustration taken from page 2 of *IT*/61, August 1969). As in all business ventures, legal or otherwise, there are some sharks who will take advantage of their customers and there are others who are anxious to establish a reputation for fair dealing so as to create the demand for more business. What one will not find is an evil pusher looking for innocent children to turn on and corrupt. Most of the dealers are small-time operators who can sell all the cannabis they can get to friends and acquaintances, and who would not be interested in selling heroin, nor would they know where they could get any to sell.

IT/61, August 1-14, 1969.

IT is published fortnightly by KNULLAR (Publishing, Printing & Promotions) Ltd.

No Copyright ☞ 1969 (UPS member)
27 Endell St., London WC2.
Telephone: Editorial 01 - 836 - 3727
Distribution 836 - 3728

Back Issues: 38-49 10/- plus 4/6 in stamps.
Other back issues: details on request

DEADLINES FOR NEXT ISSUE
FIRST POST on following days:

Small Ads, Advertising,
What's Happening: August 7th
Editorial Copy: August 9th

*IT girl badges still 1/6 plus s.a.e.
Annual subscriptions (26 issues)
U.K. & Eire: £2. 12s.
Elsewhere : £3. 10s.
Air Mail: £4. 10s.

RETAIL OUTLETS:
FOR INNER LONDON VAN
DISTRIBUTION, RING 836-3728

IT no 61 dedicated to George de la Warr,
IN MEMORIAM

← ← ← ← ← ← ← ← ← ← ← ← ← ← ←

DOPE ON DOPE — LONDON —

PAKISTANI BLACK

£110-115	per weight
£ 55-60	per half-weight
£ 10	per oz.

Make sure when buying that the inside is smooth — no grit, rubber, etc. If it's pure it's the best smoke on the Interzone market at the moment / Zappy clear-headed stuff / Releases lots of energy / Tendency not to sleep.

DARK BROWN LEBANESE

£100 - 110	per weight
£ 50 - 55	per half-weight
£ 10	per oz.

Weight arrives bound in cloth with government stamp on. Heavy smoke/ Tendency to fall out after few joints if not moving around/ Get pretty high on it.

RED LEBANESE

£100	per weight
£ 50	per half-weight
£ 10	per oz.

A lower quality hashish. Hash pollen being passed off as Red Lebanese and that's an even lousier smoke.

MOROCCAN KIEF

£10	per oz.

Not much around: Certainly up with the best hash/ Very good smoke.

Two weeks. OK
don't mean it. Each
beaten up by fuz, in
being exclusively I
no sympathy for
you.

We repeat
use your bra
once, quit r
smashed b
useless li

THER
Greece,
hashish,
were wok
off the be
taken in ur
days withot
cation privilu
out formal ch.

While this l
procedures, the
attitude taken b
Athens — 'they a
course they would
'if they're from M
are guilty'. But t
tourist season
it costs mor
days, the
plane f
arrange
etically
made.

Either
help prot
the Ameri
come at th
totally indi
kids are fac
matter of f
than all be
charged an
reason at a
appreciate
one in any
senators, i

5 The Controversial Problems

Social Implications

The social aspects of cannabis are much more important than the medical problems. The unspoken fact is that doctors really do not know much about cannabis. It is not used as a therapeutic drug and the regular user does not come to the notice of the medical profession. The doctors see only those who need psychiatric treatment for reasons other than smoking pot, or the ex-smoker who is now a heroin addict, or the unlucky smoker who has been arrested. But most people who smoke pot have no need of psychiatric treatment and with a bit of luck will not get arrested.

It is only to be expected that public concern and individual suffering will tend to concentrate the attention of social workers and doctors on to those areas of the social scene where young people are in trouble. But we must not be misled by this. There is a far greater number of young people, including many who take cannabis, who have problems that do not give rise to anxiety, or who have no problem at all. As yet there does not exist a reliable and representative study of British cannabis users who have never been under treatment or arrest. Therefore our knowledge about the social implications of cannabis is scanty.

For every person who is arrested for possessing cannabis there are hundreds that are undetected. Any law which acts more like a lucky dip than an enforcement policy is a questionable law, especially when a particular segment of the population (e.g. coloured immigrants) are more likely to be caught. It is also alleged that the law is the cause of bad police practices and the development of a growing alienation between young people and the police. In the last two years, 7,754 people were arrested for cannabis offences and about a quarter of these were sent to prison (or borstal, detention centre or approved school). The financial cost of the administration of such a law deserves to be questioned. An analysis of the figures given in the Wootton report shows that almost 1,000 (990 under the age of twenty-one) young people were arrested in one year alone; most of them (782) were first offenders. The social cost of 'criminalizing' these adolescents must be queried.

It is a very important social fact that cannabis appeals mostly to the younger generations. The total number of users (however many that may be) is not a large proportion of the total population, but it may well be a significant segment of those under the age of thirty. It is also said that this is the drug above all others that appeals to an articulate group that is anti-authority and in revolt against the older generations. Others have suggested that cannabis is simply the latest fashion in non-conformism, and will be superseded by a new craze when the next generation arrives on the scene. But some talented young artists and composers have made claims for the positive effect of cannabis on creativity and these deserve to be examined carefully and impartially.

The rapid spread of cannabis to other middle-class users and students is an interesting sociological phenomenon. It is these people who provide the articulate arguments in favour of cannabis. They are not convinced that the law is based on scientific evidence about what this drug does to those who use it. Some of these people have carried on a well publicized campaign in favour of the legalization of cannabis. The now famous advertisement which appeared in *The Times* in 1967 was signed by many well-known people and quoted opinions from doctors respected in their profession. This advertisement was not a direct plea for legalization, as many people seem to assume, but a petition to the Home Secretary advocating cannabis law reform.

Subsequently the Wootton report endorsed some of the reforms suggested in the advertisement and one of them is now incorporated into the new Misuse of Drugs Bill. In the last few years more and more well-known people have suggested that the dangers of cannabis may be exaggerated and the present law may be the cause of unnecessary social distress. A report from the National Council for Civil Liberties (1969) has drawn attention to the erosion of citizens' rights in the way the drug laws are being enforced.

In the last few years the debate on the social effects of cannabis has continued in Parliament, the press and elsewhere. Some of the main arguments against cannabis are:

(1) That it can act as a stepping stone to the truly addictive drugs; the reasons for this are said to be sociological rather than physiological.

(2) That it leads to other forms of crime.

(3) That it encourages sexual misconduct and other kinds of immoral behaviour.

(4) That it encourages the development of an underground group which is divisive.

All of these major controversies are discussed in detail in later chapters.[1] An even greater sociological mystery is why people are so illogical about recreational drugs. If being stoned is so wicked, why is being drunk so funny? It sometimes happens that the very people who are demanding that drug takers should be severely punished are themselves taking drugs to calm them down, give them energy or help them slim.

Cannabis and Other Drugs

Public attitudes to psychoactive drugs are not very sensible or consistent. Until recently most people confused all drug users with the stereotype of the junkie. Over the last four chapters I have attempted to show that there are important variations in the way these drugs take effect. In particular there are fundamental differences between cannabis and the other recreational drugs.

Amphetamines are widely prescribed and are used by young and old. Unlike cannabis most of the misuse is with pills which have been obtained legally. Tolerance, dependence and psychosis are recognized consequences of using amphetamines. Similar hazards do not result from using cannabis.

1. See chapters 9–12.

Barbiturates are socially accepted and widely prescribed. Unlike cannabis, they are capable of producing tolerance, dependence and death. More old people use barbiturates than young people use pot.

LSD is much stronger than cannabis. Even the experienced user of LSD may find himself in difficulties because the response is so intense and variable, whereas pot permits a more dependable controlled usage. Furthermore there are reports of dangerously deluded states and possible genetic effects as a result of taking LSD, both of which are unknown to those who take cannabis.

Opiates and in particular *heroin* produce tolerance, whereas cannabis users do not have to increase the dose to get the same effect. Unlike heroin, cannabis does not cause physical dependence and withdrawal effects do not occur when its use is discontinued. Over-dosage of heroin and other hard drugs may result in death; pneumonia, malnutrition, infection and general ill-health are frequent consequences, but these hazards are not found in users of cannabis. The heroin addict soon gets drawn into a junkie sub-culture where obtaining the drug becomes a way of life. Most cannabis users do not form aberrant social groups, although some do, but even in these groups drug use is only a part of adolescent alienation and not the sole purpose of the group.

Alcohol is often compared with cannabis and indeed there are many similarities. Both are used to help a person to relax and to remove social handicaps such as nervousness or reserve. Both dull inhibitions so that caution vanishes for a while. But cannabis does not induce tolerance, does not cause physical damage to the body tissues and does not enhance the effects of barbiturates and other drugs, whereas alcohol does all these things. When taken in excess, the drinker may become aggressive but the cannabis user becomes passive. The drinker often gets a hangover, a very rare experience for the user of cannabis. But the principal difference is that alcohol is legal. Axiomatic this may be, but many of the most important differences stem from this fact. Alcohol can be drunk by people who respect the established conventions, but cannabis appeals to a group that is anti-authority. We have devised social controls for alcohol and feel that we know how to deal with it.

Moreover we are able to enforce these controls because we have learnt how to detect the presence of alcohol in the human body. We have not yet devised a chemical test to determine the extent of intoxication by cannabis.[2] Even by straightforward observations, it is far more difficult to identify the man under the influence of pot than the man under the influence of alcohol. But of course the main reason why it is easier to spot the user of alcohol is because the behaviour of the cannabis user is much less disruptive to those who are near him.

Tobacco is the most widely used addictive drug in this country. Most smokers would find it extremely hard to give up the habit and even those who say they use tobacco only because they enjoy it are probably disguising an addiction which has taken control of their will power. At the 1970 congress of the Royal Society of Health, it was condemned by the Government's Chief Medical Officer as 'the biggest noxious influence in our environment'. It is sometimes said that the Government cannot restrict cigarette smoking because so much money is raised by taxation; but it is estimated that one fifth of all absences from work for illness can be connected in some way with cigarette smoking and ten per cent of all deaths can be attributed, directly or indirectly, to tobacco; therefore it is possible that the cost to the National Health Service is greater than the money raised by taxing tobacco. The short-term effects are substantially harmless, but it is now known that the long-term smoking of cigarettes induces cancer of the lung, exacerbates chronic bronchitis and is a contributory cause of coronary thrombosis. None of these dangers were apparent even after people had been smoking for hundreds of years, so this is a warning that one day we may find hitherto unknown drawbacks in cannabis. But this warning must apply to very many substances, particularly new chemicals such as monosodium glutamate (used to season food), the residue of pesticides in fruit and vegetables, petrol fumes which cause atmospheric pollution and even certain cosmetic creams.[3]

2. It is likely that a satisfactory urine test will become available before long (Christiansen, 1969).
3. One cream advertised as a bust developer might cause tumours and

It would be absurd to refuse to make use of new chemical discoveries because we are unable to provide certain proof that they are harmless. Even if we can show that a particular substance is harmful upon occasions, we still have to weigh the advantages against the drawbacks. It may be possible to show that the contraceptive pill increases the risks of thrombosis in a very few and is the cause of less serious side-effects in others. But most people would feel the benefits of the pill far outweigh the disadvantages. It is often said that there are no similar advantages to cannabis as it has no therapeutic use, but a drug which gives so much pleasure and has so many advocates cannot be written off as valueless.

---

disturb a woman's menstrual periods, according to a report from a consultant toxicologist in the Government's Consumer Council periodical (*Focus*, December 1967).

The Early Days

Cannabis has been taken for hundreds of years in India and the Middle East, but it is only very recently that it has become a problem in this country. Except for the areas bordering directly on the Mediterranean, there was very little interest in cannabis in Europe. Although the famous Club des Hachichins was established in Paris, Gautier and his friends were thought to be a very eccentric group and the use of hashish did not spread.

After the cultivation of hemp was abandoned in America, the remaining plants were allowed to go to seed and became weeds which spread across the United States. But it was not until this century that a new generation found a use for this prolific plant. It was the Mexican labourers who introduced the idea of smoking it. By 1926 cannabis was well known in New Orleans and gradually its use spread to all the large urban areas of the United States. At first it was mainly consumed by Mexicans, Negroes and Puerto Ricans – the minority groups living in poverty in the large cities. In some ways these people were similar to the users in Arabic countries who found that cannabis could bring comfort and relief from the hard living conditions of the very poor.

But then a strange phenomenon developed. Instead of the habit spreading gradually up the social scale which might not have been unexpected, what happened was a new interest in cannabis among a quite different section of the community. At first a small group of intellectuals, stimulated by the writings of Aldous Huxley (1959), tried experiments with mescaline and cannabis. But from 1960 onwards the development of the civil rights and then the hippy movements gave impetus to this interest and marihuana became the subject of much speculation and discussion among middle-class students, university staff, entertainers and artists. For the first time there were a number of articulate voices who questioned the old assumptions about cannabis.

But before this happened the US Government had already made it illegal by passing the Federal Marihuana Tax Act which effectively prohibits the use of the drug. This was in response to public demand starting about 1930 when the popular press began to create and spread a number of myths about marihuana. For some reason sensational stories about this drug have always been thought by editors to be good news stories which will sell papers. The series of myths which were circulated forty years ago in America are still used even today to support arguments against the use of marihuana.

Similar alarming and picturesque stories appeared in British newspapers from time to time. One of the earliest examples was in the *Daily Mirror* on 24 July 1939. Under the long headline 'Just a cigarette you'd think, but it was made from a sinister weed and an innocent girl falls victim of this TERROR', this full-page article contains most of the famous marihuana myths.

The idea that it is addictive:

In London there are thousands of them. Young girls, once beautiful, whose thin faces show the ravages of the weed they started smoking for a thrill. Young men who, in the throes of a hangover from the drug, find their only relief in dragging at yet another marihuana cigarette.

The stories about cannabis leading to violence and other reactions which are the exact opposite to the known medical effects; the reference to abnormal 'strength' suggests that the reporter got this from a description of the effects of cocaine:

One girl, just over twenty, known among her friends for her quietness and modesty, suddenly threw all caution to the winds. She began staying out late at nights. Her parents became anxious when she began to walk about the house without clothes. They stopped her when she attempted to go into the street like that. At times she became violent and showed abnormal strength. Then she would flop down in a corner, weeping and crouching like an animal.

Just a cigarette, you'd think, but it was made from a sinister weed and an innocent girl falls victim to this

TERROR!

MARIHUANA ...

Does that word mean anything to you?

Perhaps you have heard vaguely that marihuana is a plant that is made into a drug.

But do you know that in every city in this country there are addicts of this dangerous drug?

In London there are thousands of them.

Young girls, once beautiful, whose thin faces show the ravages of the weed they started smoking for a thrill.

Young men who, in the throes of a hangover from the drug, find their only relief in dragging at yet another marihuana cigarette.

How do they obtain this drug—since the police are hot on the trail of all suspected traffickers?

They obtain it from so many unexpected sources that as fast as one is closed by the police, so another opens up. "Night clubs, reputable hotels and cafes are frequented by agents. They operate from the least likely places—milliner's shops, hairdressers, antique shops.

But in Soho, in little lodging houses run by coloured men and women, the cigarette can be had for a secret password, and a very small sum of money.

And many terrible tales are told about marihuana addicts.

One girl, just over twenty, known among her friends for her quietness and modesty, suddenly threw all caution to the winds.

She began staying out late at nights. Her parents became anxious when she began to walk about the house without clothes. They stopped her when she attempted to go into the street like that.

At times she became violent and showed abnormal strength. Then she would flop down in a corner, weeping and crouching like an animal. Soon she left home.

No trace could be found of her, but cigarettes and ends in her room were identified as marihuana.

How much does a marihuana cigarette cost? Just a shilling!

Or in a "reefer club," the low haunts where men, usually coloured, sell the cigarette, a puff can be had for sixpence. The fumes of the smoke are caressing, but they leave a somewhat acrid taste and a pungent, sickly smell.

That is, to the beginner. The addict likes it. She likes it, not because of its taste or smell, but because it gives her abnormal strength and makes her indifferent to her surroundings.

One day, passing a narrow street in Soho, I saw a small crowd gazing at the third floor of a dingy house.

A young and lovely woman, her clothes in shreds, stood perilously perched on a window ledge.

Behind her was a man. He, too, was wild-looking and dishevelled. Several times the girl made an effort to jump and the man feebly held her back.

Soon, a third man appeared, coloured and strong, and hauled them both back. They were both marihuana addicts.

As she disappeared, she could be heard screaming: "I can fly. Well, I don't care if I die!"

Unconscious of herself, of any danger, she acted on the impulse to do the impossible.

I heard of one case, a nineteen-year-old dancing girl who was taken to a "reefer club" by a party of friends.

Soon a man was at her side, offering her a cigarette, for which he made no charge. It was a decoy.

Soon she became one of his best customers, spending half her salary on the weed.

She sank lower and lower. Her associates became criminals, drug lunatics, and dope peddlers.

Unlike opium, hashish and other drugs which make their victims seek solitude,

marihuana drives its victims into society, forcing them to violence, often murder.

One man, in the delusion that his limbs were going to be cut off, killed his mother, father, brother and two sisters with an axe.

Another man would speak of people trying to corner him and hurl daggers at him. His sense of time, space and taste was distorted.

The seeds is found in most hemp and bird seeds.

It isn't hard to make marihuana cigarettes. The plant is dried before a fire or the sun for a few days. The leaves are then chopped up and mixed with ordinary tobacco.

Marihuana alone would be enough to kill the average man. Then they are loosely rolled into cigarettes, slightly shorter than the normal.

For women, the menace of the cigarette is greater than for men.

Here is a true story that illustrates this fact.

A girl of twenty-one was persuaded by an older man to elope with him.

For months her father searched vainly for his daughter. One night he saw a girl, her eyes staring wildly in front of her, her hands drooping, her head leaning on a man's shoulder.

He was horrified, but even more horrified when a second glance told him that this was his daughter, ravaged by neglect and ill-use.

"I am not going home. I'm going to America," she wailed, when she saw her father.

The man with her refused to give her up. The girl clung fiercely to him.

There might have been a brawl but the father said:

"I have a friend outside who will call the police if I'm not outside with my daughter in ten minutes."

Reluctantly his daughter went with him. In a few months she was cured of those nightmare weeks.

It may happen to any man or woman. The next victim may be your best friend.

A cigarette seems harmless enough. It is not so easy to check the craving.

For marihuana can turn happy lives into hell.

E. S.

T—C

The well-known stories about drug users leaping from windows, usually told about LSD nowadays:

A young and lovely woman, her clothes in shreds, stood perilously perched on a window ledge. Behind her was a man. He, too, was wild-looking and dishevelled. Several times the girl made an effort to jump and the man feebly held her back. Soon a third man appeared, coloured and strong, and hauled them both back. They were both marihuana addicts.

The suggestion that the traffickers are coloured:

But in Soho, in little lodging houses run by coloured men and women, the cigarette can be had for a secret password, and a very small sum of money.

The fable that a person can smoke cannabis and be hooked on it without realizing it:

I have heard of one case, a nineteen-year old dancing girl who was taken to a 'reefer club' by a party of friends. Soon a man was at her side, offering her a cigarette. It was a decoy. Soon she became one of his best customers, spending half her salary on the weed.

The confusion with other drugs:

Unlike opium, hashish [sic] and other drugs which make their victims seek solitude, marihuana drives its victims into society, forcing them to violence, even murder.

And inevitably the suggestion that marihuana and irresistible sexual desires are linked together:

For women, the menace of the cigarette is greater than for men. A girl of twenty-one was persuaded by a coloured man to elope with him

All of these myths have been repeated time and again over the thirty years since this story first appeared. There are, of course, many serious arguments against the use of cannabis (and these are studied in detail in later chapters). But every informed person knows that cannabis is not addictive, does not make the user suicidal, is not sold only by coloured people, cannot be disguised as ordinary tobacco, does not drive users to violence and murder, and is not an aphrodisiac.

Newmark (1968) gives several examples of sensational press items about drugs:

'The problem of drugs is the worst we have had to face since the Black Death.' Speaker at the General Assembly of the Church of Scotland.

'LONDON SETS DRUG WATCH IN SCHOOLS. "Happening all over the place" – A doctor.'

Actually the doctor said that as yet he had no evidence of widespread drug taking in schools but he had his suspicions.

A well-known writer in the *Daily Express* wrote '. . . Dr Plumb . . . has just written in the *Spectator* arguing that drug taking should be legalized.' In fact Dr Plumb, a professor of history at Cambridge, suggested that after suitable research it might turn out to be more sensible to permit the use of cannabis (not all drug taking) rather than ban it.

The press still tends to treat all drugs as though they had the same effects and were equally dangerous. When the report on amphetamines and LSD was published in March 1970, several newspapers summarized the recommendations as if they applied to all drugs and quoted figures for the number of heroin addicts which were quite irrelevant. 'HIDDEN MENACE OF DRUGGED DRIVERS' in the *Evening Standard* referred to anti-histamines used to relieve travel sickness, not to illegal drugs. In January 1968 the *Guardian* had a headline: 'MARIJUANA AND LSD COULD RESULT IN "MONSTER CHILDREN".'

Alex Mitchell (1969), a reporter on the *Sunday Times*, noted that the *Daily Express* in 1967 reported that 'students bought drugs from an attractive Swedish blonde at undergraduate parties'. Mitchell wondered 'whether she was the same girl who cropped up in a *Daily Telegraph* article almost three years earlier' when it reported that a group was 'organizing the manufacture of reefers for Cambridge undergraduates. They are believed to include a West Indian, a Frenchman and a blonde Swedish girl.' Mitchell adds: 'Needless to say the Baltic beauty was never named: she remains a part of the drug mythology which Fleet Street has constructed over the past ten years. . . . Exploring the cuttings covering five decades revealed an unbelievably shallow approach to the reporting of drug affairs.'

In fact there was no drug problem of any kind in Great Britain before 1914. It was something the Chinese did in Limehouse. When the Egyptians first demanded that the drug should be put under international control in 1924, the British reaction was not untypical. They suggested a committee to study the situation, but they were overruled and so controls were introduced in Britain in 1928 in order to implement an international agreement.

But cannabis was not a British problem at that time. The highest pre-war figure for cannabis offences was 18 and this was in 1938. About twenty years ago the Customs found that increasing quantities were being brought into the country, mostly by immigrants; at first the chief offenders were West African, but later there were more West Indians.

In 1950 there were over a hundred prosecutions for cannabis offences for the very first time. This was the result of a series of raids on certain London jazz clubs and it became clear that cannabis was now being used by Englishmen as well as by immigrants. But it was not until 1964 that there were more white people than coloured being convicted of possessing cannabis. Today there are three times as many white as coloured offenders.

Middle-Class Users

In one important aspect the spread of cannabis in Britain differs fundamentally from the American experience. In this country cannabis has never been the favourite drug of the poverty-stricken and undernourished. There is no equivalent in Britain to the poor hashish users in Arabic and Asian countries or the Mexicans, Puerto Ricans and Negroes smoking marihuana in the large urban communities of America. The deprived in Britain stick to alcohol, and the down and out to methylated spirits. It is true there were the same scare stories in the press as in America, and the same sudden middle-class interest among students and intellectuals, but the original smokers in this country, the seamen and musicians, were not from the depressed classes. Thus there is no history of extensive cannabis misuse among the very poor and social workers do not associate this drug with the criminal fringe, the psychopaths and others with severe personality disorders.

Even now cannabis is not the main illegal drug for working-class users. People from the depressed areas in this country are more likely to use amphetamines, even though this drug is harder to obtain. Pep pills are also the favoured drug in the criminal sub-cultures. Scott and Willcox (1965) found evidence of amphetamines in urine tests in 17 per cent of admissions to remand homes. No doubt some people have taken cannabis before committing a crime, but it is unlikely to be helpful; amphetamines increase courage and energy, but a man under the influence of cannabis prefers to sit still and enjoy himself passively.

A British criminologist (Downes, 1966) noted that the British user of cannabis was 'hip', middle class or student class. An American writer (Chein, 1964) agrees that the interest in cannabis in Great Britain tends to spread down, not up, the socio-economic scale. The cannabis users during the 1967–8 hippy movement were rarely working-class youths; these articulate proselytizers were more likely to be drop outs from grammar schools and colleges.

Until recently middle-class boys and girls were influenced hardly at all by the new working-class youth movements. The era of rock and roll, starting with Bill Haley and the Comets in the late 1950s, was brash and aggressive. The spread of pep pills started during the days of the teddy boys and the racial explosions in Notting Hill and Nottingham. From this came the mods on their scooters and the rockers on their motor cycles meeting and fighting on the beaches at Southend, Brighton and other holiday resorts. It was a restless violent period when youth clubs and cinemas were smashed for enjoyment, but it had little to do with the politically committed activities of CND and the later student demonstrations.

The present-day successors to the rockers are probably the Hell's Angels, the Californian gangs of outlaw motor cyclists who have established a few chapters (or units) in the South of England. A similar, more recent, phenomenon is the gangs of young working-class boys called 'skinheads', an inelegant, strangely puritanical group who go out to cause 'agro' – a skinhead term for aggravation and violence. But these movements attract only a minority of the young people of today. For many others the swinging teenage scene is represented by the stars of pop music and the new hair styles and bright fast-changing fashions in clothes. At the other end of the spectrum is the 'underground' or 'alternative society', the movement which developed from the beats, and later the hippies. Stimulants and violence are quite alien to this new teenage cult. This is a rebellion against authority and materialism, but it is also a thoughtful search for new values in which cannabis plays a part.

The Underground

Cannabis has also been associated with the development of new forms of folk music and contemporary art. Whereas the amphetamines attracted the rockers and their successors because the pills energized and stimulated the physical capacities, cannabis seems to have greater effects in the spiritual sphere, increasing the inward-directed mental faculties. It is a drug of contemplation and peace. This is why it is particularly attractive to those in the psychedelic sub-culture (Brickman, 1968). Cannabis is their favourite drug because its effects reflect the desire for tranquillity and non-violence and it is popular in the Eastern countries whose philosophies have encouraged the people in the underground to take a fresh approach to religion.

But it would be unfair to suggest that the underground is only concerned with cannabis and drugs. It is a genuine protest against present-day materialist values, with a special interest in the mystical elements of life. Leech (1969) in a Christian analysis of this sub-culture writes: 'It is a serious movement with a concern for new values based on love, and it has brought about what can only be described as a new spirituality.' It is ironic that these young people without religious affiliations are interested in the transcendental aspects of religion at a time when Christians, particularly the 'new theologians', are turning away from this towards reasoned intellectual problems.

The underground also has serious social and political aims, expressed vehemently and passionately in *IT, OZ, Black Dwarf* and other periodicals which provide the movement with focus and cohesion. *IT* has a circulation of 48,000 and must be read by more than twice that number.

Silberman (1967) thinks that cannabis

enjoys particular popularity among those who, for one reason or another, are unable or unwilling to participate in anything in regard to which the possession of a well-developed drive for power would be of great importance. In ideological terms it would be true to say that it is the drug of those whose general orientation is anti-authoritarian, anti-militaristic and, in the context of contemporary Western societies, anti-establishment.

Work on the underground is a 'hustle' or 'gig' which are words used for any non-violent means of making money which does not require regularity or taking orders from supervisors without question. 'Greys' are the people who work for wages until they get a pension. None the less several excellent self-help organizations, such as Bit and Release, have grown from this movement.

Bit is a two-way information service for young people who cannot get on terms with the existing organs of our society. It started in the summer of 1968 as a simple information service but people soon made it much more than that. On average, London Bit answers over 1,200 inquiries a week, mostly by telephone. 'People want pads, jobs, advice, help. And we've got to give it to them. The pregnant chicks are ours, the people with nowhere to live are ours, the people using drugs are ours, the failures are ours and the losers are ours too.' This is from an advertisement for Bit, which is essentially a twenty-four-hour-a-day, seven-day-a-week, advisory bureau and emergency service for unattached young people, operating from an office provided by Westminster City Council. Bit was conceived as self-help and many of the 200 voluntary workers are from among those who have been helped.

Release was established to help those who have been arrested for drug offences and to arrange for them to be represented by lawyers who have experience of such cases. Advice is given on individual rights regarding searches, arrests, court procedures and the interpretation of the law. Financial assistance is provided in those cases where legal aid has been refused, and medical attention, work or accommodation is arranged for those who need it. Release is run entirely by young people and a report of the work done since it started in 1967 (Coon and Harris, 1969) showed that in one year 603 people had been helped; 364 (60 per cent) of these were cannabis users.

These and other self-help organizations are set up to help these young people, including many who take cannabis, to find their way in a society with which they are unsympathetic but in which they must live. There are others who take this social alienation to its logical end and try to live their own lives without contributing to or taking anything from the community around them. In fact this is very difficult to do as our society tends to be all-embracing. These people find it very hard to keep their independence and despite their best resolution they become aware that they are dependent on the state and its ramifications. The ideal of cutting off from materialist society is occasionally attained in self-contained rural settlements founded in the United States; in general our climate makes such enterprises very hard and unattractive.

It is important to note that the psychedelic underground is quite distinct from the hard drug scene or from the Soho drug sub-culture. It has hardly any similarities with the purple-heart craze of a few years ago, nor is it connected with the amphetamine users to be found in Soho and the East End of London. The 1968 outbreak of injecting methedrine (an amphetamine obtainable in ampoules and known as 'speed' in the drug world) spread from central London to distant towns, and for the first time provided a link between the 'pill heads' (amphetamine users) and the 'junkies' (heroin addicts). But very few cannabis users were involved and *IT* and other underground publications campaigned vigorously against it with slogans like 'SPEED KILLS'.

Other Users

The young people of the underground are the best-known users of cannabis, but they are not the only ones. There are many more who smoke hash for pleasure at week-ends as their equivalent to other people's alcohol. They do not join campaigns to legalize pot, nor are they articulate defenders of the drug. Consequently they are harder to identify.

Most people agree that a large number of immigrants use cannabis, but it is very difficult to get any idea of the actual numbers or the proportion within each immigrant group that takes this drug. Although it is illegal to use cannabis in most African and the Caribbean countries, its use is traditional and it is not usually prosecuted unless it is practised very openly. It is generally regarded as a pardonable and not very serious fault, so it is not surprising that many do not give up the habit when they come here. Some immigrants from Cyprus, Malta and Pakistan also use cannabis. It is not true, however, that the majority of coloured men smoke pot. The Wootton committee did not find any clear link between immigration and cannabis smoking.

The Wootton committee also reported that there was a growing number of workers among the unskilled occupations who were using cannabis; these people were said to be industrious and law-abiding. But there were others who had dropped out of the educational system and were actively rebellious. Some of these people avoided any kind of regular work and were often in trouble with the law. But very few of this group kept exclusively to cannabis. They tended to be severely disturbed and were prepared to take any drug they could find. This multiple-drug use nearly always includes cannabis because it is one of the easiest drugs to obtain, but it is a mistake to confuse these junkies with people who only smoke pot.

Unfortunately there has been no research which helps to give a description of the cannabis users in Britain. In an investigation in Oakland, California, a group of young people were firm in their conviction, based on their own experience, that marihuana resulted in harmless pleasure and increasing conviviality, did not lead to violence, madness or addiction, was less harmful than alcohol, and could be regulated. They cited case after case of individuals known to them who had not been harmed in health, school achievement, athletics or career as a result of smoking cannabis; and they were not themselves interested in being helped to abstain from the drug. The investigators (Blumer and associates at the University of California) make the important point that these young people are not opting out; on the contrary they are making a positive effort to conform with the accepted activities of others in their group. The investigators conclude that youthful cannabis use in Oakland is an extensive and deeply rooted practice, 'and is buttressed by a body of justifying beliefs and convictions, involves a repertoire of practical knowledge and incorporates a body of precautions against apprehension or arrest. Drug use constitutes for the users a natural way of life and does not represent a pathological phenomenon.'

A similar study in this country would probably disclose areas where the use of cannabis is now socially accepted in the same way as in Oakland. But there are many more areas where any kind of drug use apart from alcohol and tobacco are denounced as dangerous behaviour.

The only certain indication of these opposing views is age. There are very few men or women over the age of forty who use cannabis, and most people who smoke pot are nearer twenty than thirty. This is a most unfortunate division in the generations which inevitably brings accusations about immaturity on one side, and complaints about repression from inflexible fuddy-duddies on the other side. It is exactly because older adults cannot look back at youthful personal experiences of cannabis (as they can at other youthful indiscretions) that they must be most careful not to misjudge the situation or jump to unfounded conclusions.

7   The Wootton Report

Other Reports

At first Government committees were only concerned with the opiates, and in particular with heroin addiction. The two reports of the Interdepartmental Committee under Lord Brain in 1961 and 1965 hardly mentioned cannabis. In the first report the committee decided that cannabis was not within their terms of reference and concluded: 'In our view cannabis is not a drug of addiction; it is an intoxicant.' In the second report they noted briefly that there is 'a risk that young people may be persuaded to turn to cannabis', which was something of an understatement even in 1965.

One important recommendation in the second Brain report was to set up a Standing Advisory Committee to keep under review the whole problem of drug dependence. As this was not a static but a changing problem, it would be helpful to bring together a group of experts with authority to advise on the social as well as the medical aspects. This committee was set up early in 1967 under the Chairmanship of Sir Edward Wayne, MD, PH D, DSC, FRCP, FRCP(G). Twenty-two other members were appointed, nine of whom were doctors. A small secretariat was formed to help the committee, but there was no money to pay for research and no special facilities. Some of the members were doctors treating addicts, but most of them had only a limited amount of knowledge of drugs although all of them have learnt over the years.

Without the facilities to initiate or carry out research, this committee cannot be expected to provide new facts or make important discoveries. All that the members can do is to discuss the matter between themselves and listen from time to time to witnesses called to give evidence because they are experts in some particular aspect of drug use. But nearly everyone who gives evidence to this committee does so as a representative of an organization which has a special interest in drugs. Conflicting views will be heard from the representatives of other organizations. The function of the committee is essentially judicial and its purpose is to reconcile the conflicting claims of its witnesses. As there is a wide variety of opinion represented among the members, the suggested solutions to the various problems of drug dependence are obtained by compromising between opposing views. The reports which are issued from time to time usually consist of an aggregation of existing opinions, including those of the chairman, the committee members, and the witnesses. A research team of three or four people working full time is more likely to produce more penetrating and workable solutions to the problems of drug use than a committee of prominent citizens meeting three or four times a year to compile and select from conflicting expert opinions.

None the less the committee has been able to give useful advice to the Home Office and Ministry of Social Security on the best way to implement the earlier recommendations of the Brain committee. Treatment centres for heroin addicts have been set up and special arrangements were introduced to control the outbreak of methedrine injections. Perhaps the most important work has been done in the sub-committees which have met more regularly than the main committee. There have been sub-committees on rehabilitation,[1] and health education,[2] amphetamines, LSD and powers of search and arrest.[3]

In April 1967 a special sub-committee was appointed to review the available evidence on the pharmacological, clinical, pathological, social and legal aspects of cannabis. After seventeen meetings under the chairmanship of the Baroness Wootton, the sub-committee's report was published in January 1969.

1. Published as a report by HMSO in 1969.
2. The results were circularized by the Department of Education.
3. These reports were published by HMSO in 1970.

The Recommendations

(1) *We recommend that in the interest of public health, it is necessary for the time being to maintain restrictions on the availability of cannabis.* Although it is stated in the report that the consumption of cannabis in moderate doses has no harmful effects, the committee felt less sure about the mental effects. This recommendation, therefore, is intended to be a temporary measure and should be reviewed from time to time, when more is known about the effects as a result of medical and social research. Meanwhile the courts should recognize that there is considerable variation in the personalities and motives of people who use cannabis.

(2) *Every encouragement, both academic and financial, should be given to suitable projects for inquiry into the cannabis problem.* It follows that if there is a lack of information on an important and controversial problem, every effort should be made to provide research facilities. Although three working parties have been set up by the Medical Research Council and an Institute for the Study of Drug Dependence has been established, progress is very slow. It is inevitable that research into drug use will be a lengthy business, but it is disquietening that even three years after the formation of the Government's Advisory Committee, very few large-scale research projects had even been started.

In March 1970 the Home Office issued a list of research on drug dependence. This list contained ten biochemical and pharmacological studies, mainly concerned with the development of techniques for detecting cannabis in the body. There were no cannabis studies listed under the clinical and treatment section. Five studies were listed under the social and psychological section; three of these were to be carried out by doctors[4] who had written papers strongly opposed to the use of cannabis even before starting the research; only one of the five has been undertaken by a sociologist. So far the Social Science Research Council has not supported any researches on the use of cannabis even though it is in the area of sociology that we most need information.

The Wootton committee found that it was impossible to estimate

4. Chapple (1966); Paton (1968); Tylden (1968).

the number of people who used cannabis and the guesses seem to range between 30,000 and 300,000. It is clearly impossible to make sense of statements about the social consequences of widespread use of cannabis until there are some reliable estimates of the prevalence of regular users. No detailed information is available about the extent of cannabis use by immigrants. There is an immediate need for sociological and psychological studies to define the different social groups and to describe the personalities of people who smoke cannabis. People do not hesitate to criticize the young for taking drugs, but in fact no one knows how many adolescents do take cannabis, how many use the drug only occasionally at parties and week-ends, and how many take it regularly. Only a well-planned research would show if there are differentiating characteristics between users who take only cannabis, and people who used to take cannabis but have now given up all drug use. Pharmacological research can also help to take away the emphasis on possession and substitute the more important criterion of use or abuse. It is possible to detect the presence of amphetamines in the body by analysis of the urine so it would now be possible to frame a law so that a person is penalized, not for possessing pep pills, but for misbehaving while under the influence of these drugs. Such a criterion cannot be used for cannabis until research workers have developed chemical tests, both qualitative and quantitative, to detect the presence of cannabis and its metabolites in the body fluids of users.

(3) *The law should progressively be recast to give Parliament greater flexibility of control over individual drugs*. This was one of the few recommendations which the Home Secretary found acceptable, although it seems likely that he does not interpret 'greater flexibility of control' in the same sense as the Wootton Committee. Mr Callaghan, speaking during the debate on the Wootton report, said that he would put before the House proposals which would give him more power to handle the problem in a much more flexible manner. He then went on to criticize the limitations of the 1964 Drugs Act which in fact does not apply to cannabis. He wanted the power to bring new synthetic drugs under the Act as they were developed and became popular with

users, and he also mentioned the need to have stronger legal control
over manufacturers, doctors, chemists and others who distribute
the drugs. He felt that there was 'a clear risk that each new fashion
of drug taking will find new gaps in the defences, which will only be
plugged too late' and the solution would be 'to have a single
comprehensive code which would rationalize and strengthen the
Government's powers'.[5]

There is much substance in Mr Callaghan's remarks about the
changing fashions in the drug scene but this has nothing to do with
the Wootton report which is about cannabis, a drug that is already
fashionable and is hardly ever prescribed by medical men. It is
difficult to see what the Home Secretary's call for new legislation
has to do with cannabis unless he feels that one illegal drug is much
like another, an attitude of mind that Lady Wootton and her
colleagues were most anxious to alter.

The Wootton committee suggested changes in the law because
there is now a better understanding of the reasons why people use
drugs. Criminological studies have cast doubts on the effectiveness
of deterrents and the general law on the treatment of offenders has
been changed considerably. The committee felt that 'the penalties
for cannabis offences have gone unreviewed for too long'. Their
idea of flexibility was that the penalties should be adjusted according to the dangers of the drug and the way it is misused.

(4) *The association in legislation of cannabis with heroin and the
other opiates is inappropriate and new legislation to deal specially
and separately with cannabis and its synthetic derivatives should be
introduced as soon as possible.* There are two reasons for this. Many
people agree that the confusion between heroin and cannabis leads
to misunderstandings and, in some cases, to injustice. The committee also stated quite clearly that the present penalties for possession
of cannabis were altogether too high. The Government accepted
the third recommendation for reasons other than those given by
the committee, and after some hesitation, the fourth recommendation was also incorporated into the new Bill, although the penalties
for possessing cannabis are still severe.

(5) *Unlawful possession of cannabis without knowledge should not*

5. From *Hansard*, 27 January 1969, column 967.

be an offence for which the law provides no defence. The practicability of distinguishing between possession intended for use and possession intended for supply should be examined. This brings to notice two of the several difficulties encountered in a law which is about possession when what we are really concerned about is the misuse of drugs. Although a recent test case was taken as far as the House of Lords, the resulting decision was by no means clear because the issues in that particular case were complex. The law should make it quite certain that a person cannot be incriminated, for example, by someone putting cannabis in his coat pocket without his knowledge.

The police maintain that it is extremely difficult to catch someone in the act of dealing in cannabis or any other drug. The unsatisfactory solution to this problem under the 1965 Act was to retain high maximum penalties for the offence of possession so that the courts could sentence a man who had been found guilty of one offence (i.e. possession) as if he had been found guilty of another (i.e. supply). It is a form of justice that is open to question; it is a bit like the bench saying to a motorist: 'You have been caught exceeding the speed limit and we have been told that you had been drinking rather heavily; however, we can't prove that you were drunk, so we are going to give you a very heavy sentence for speeding.' The proposals for the new legislation allow this practice to continue: although the new offence of 'possession with intent to supply' is introduced, a maximum penalty of five years for the possession of cannabis is proposed. It is difficult to imagine a situation where the simple possession of cannabis deserves such a severe sentence.

The new Bill distinguishes between possession and trafficking and increases the penalty for selling cannabis to a maximum of fourteen years. This reflects the public demand for heavy penalties for traffickers which is based on a misunderstanding of the role of the dealer. Nevertheless if a man is making money out of selling an illegal substance, it is reasonable to expect him to be dealt with more severely than someone who is merely using a drug.

(6) *Possession of a small amount of cannabis should not normally be regarded as a serious crime to be punished by imprisonment.* This is a very radical recommendation and one which caused a large

amount of adverse comment in the press. But informed opinion
is coming round to the idea that prison is not a sensible way to
treat people who wish to use cannabis. What even informed opinion
found it difficult to take was the quite explicit statement that
possession is not a *serious* crime. But the committee went still
further in paragraph 90 of the report, where they state that prison
is the wrong place even for those who supply on a limited scale.
They do not attempt to define what they mean by limited scale,
but even a fairly strict definition would include about nine out of
ten of the transactions between users and sellers because the
amounts involved are so small.

(7) *The offence of unlawful possession, sale or supply of cannabis
should be punishable on summary conviction with a fine not exceeding £100, or imprisonment for a term not exceeding four
months, or both such fine or imprisonment. On conviction on indictment the penalty should be an unlimited fine, or imprisonment for a
term not exceeding two years or both such fine and imprisonment.*
Thus the committee recommended quite considerable reductions
in the penalties. The penalties for possession under the 1965 Act in
force when the committee reported, the penalties in the new Bill
and the recommended penalties in the Wootton report are
summarized in the following table.

Maximum penalties	1965 Act	1970 Bill	Wootton report
Summary:			
Fine	£250	£400	£100
Imprisonment	12 months	6 months	4 months
Indictment:			
Fine	£1,000	unlimited	unlimited
Imprisonment	10 years	5 years	2 years

Some members of the committee argued strongly against any
kind of prison sentence for simple possession, but in the end were
persuaded to agree to a maximum penalty of four months imprisonment because this sentence would allow the defendant the option

of going for trial by jury and also because a prison sentence gives the judiciary the chance to deal with what the committee called 'difficult individual cases'.

The committee were aware that a substantial part of the smuggling of cannabis is in small amounts (paragraph 37) and is not exploited to any significant extent by professional criminals (paragraph 38). Therefore they expected that nearly all cases would be dealt with summarily by imposing a small fine. The reaction to this showed that it was a most unpopular recommendation. The Home Secretary and the opposition spokesman on home affairs both said that this recommendation would make it appear that Parliament was condoning the smoking of cannabis.[6]

(8) *The existing law which inhibits research requiring the smoking of cannabis (section 5, Dangerous Drugs Act, 1965) should be amended to allow qualified workers to study its use both by observation and by laboratory and social experiments.* There has been considerable uncertainty about the law on smoking cannabis for research purposes with the result that no serious study has been made in this country on the effects of smoking on humans even in laboratory conditions. As the social factors are even more important than the pharmacological problems, it is essential that researchers should be free to study these phenomena by observation and experiments outside as well as inside the laboratory without the risk of prosecution.

Although the Home Secretary gave the lack of information as the reason for rejecting many of the recommendations in the Wootton report, it was notable that he never mentioned this recommendation in his speech when the report was debated in the House of Commons. In fact this was one of the earliest and most urgent of the suggestions made by the full Standing Advisory Committee, long before the Wootton report was published. Many members realized that their work was hindered by the shortage of information that could only be obtained by fairly elaborate and

6. 'If we were to adopt what is proposed or started to take a namby-pamby attitude about it, we should need our heads examined. I range myself wholeheartedly behind the Home Secretary on this issue.' – Quintin Hogg in *Hansard*, 27 January 1969, column 957.

lengthy research. It was suggested that a short Bill should be put
before Parliament to make research on cannabis possible without
the risk of prosecution. It was thought that such a Bill would not
arouse much opposition, but the Home Office advisers to the
committee felt that this plan was not practical. They maintained
that a short Bill on the subject of research into cannabis could not
be confined to this subject and far-reaching amendments would be
added during its passage through Parliament. So it was decided to
wait until the Government was ready to introduce comprehensive
legislation into which a special clause would be included to allow
bona fide research workers to investigate the effects of smoking
cannabis. But in fact three years have been lost between the time
when the law on cannabis research might have been changed and
the introduction of this new legislation. It is possible that much
useful information could have been obtained in that time, information which would have been invaluable during the preparation of
the new Bill and the subsequent discussion of the various proposals.

(9) *Section 5 of the Dangerous Drugs Act, 1965 (permitting
premises to be used for smoking cannabis, etc.), should be redefined
in scope so as to apply to premises open to the public, to exclude the
reference to dealing in cannabis and cannabis resin, and to remove
the absolute nature of the liability on managers.* This recommendation has been partly approved by the Home Secretary in the proposals for new legislation so that occupiers and managers commit
an offence if they *knowingly* permit a drug to be used or sold in their
premises. This will obviate the liability of the landlord of private
premises who would have been convicted under the old law even if
he was able to show that he did not know that pot was being
smoked in his house. But the Home Secretary has rejected the
suggestion that this should only be an offence in public premises.

(10) *The Advisory Committee should undertake, as a matter of
urgency, a review of police powers of arrest and search in relation to
drug offences generally, with a view to advising the Secretary of
State on any changes that may be appropriate in the law, particularly
as regards cannabis.* The Wootton committee seemed to think this
task was too big for them because they felt that the question of
police powers could not be realistically considered in relation to

cannabis alone. But there is no doubt that this is a most important issue. There is a growing public concern about the way the police are using their powers of search and arrest and many youth workers see this as one of the main causes of the substantial deterioration in the relations between young people and the police.

It may be said that this recommendation is a bit timid. In a large number of cases the police search for drugs in general, but this is not true of every case. There must be occasions when the reasonable grounds for suspicion relate only to the use of cannabis; for example, it is the only drug that has a pungent smell. The very extensive police powers of search and arrest, which may be necessary for the more harmful drugs, are difficult to justify for cannabis, the possession of which, according to the report, is a relatively minor offence.

This recommendation was thought to be 'a matter of urgency' and a new sub-committee under the chairmanship of William Deedes was set up soon after the Wootton report was published. In an early debate on drugs Mr Deedes said in the House of Commons: 'It makes no sense for the police to go round raiding and stripping young people at parties to find drugs, some of which their elders treat as a staple diet. The posture against the young becomes morally untenable.' But his report turned out to be rather a disappointing document, with few positive recommendations.[7]

(11) *The development of the manufacture of synthetic cannabinols should be kept under review and, if necessary, control should be imposed under powers provided by the Pharmacy and Poisons Act, 1933, and The Drugs (Prevention of Misuse) Act, 1964.* Much progress is being made in the pharmacological study of cannabis and the active ingredient has been synthesized. It is possible that synthetic pot will be available in large quantities before long, and this substance is likely to be purer and safer, and perhaps more potent, than the product obtained from the plant. Such a substance would not be covered by the Dangerous Drugs Act of 1965, but the proposed legislation would make it possible to add new products of the pharmacological industry to the schedule of re-

7. The report of the Deedes sub-committee is discussed in more detail in chapter 13.

stricted drugs simply by regulations placed before the two Houses of Parliament.

(12) *Preparations of cannabis and its derivatives should continue to be available on prescription for purposes of medical treatment and research. Provision should be made in legislation for records to be maintained so that the position can be kept under review.* The committee did not want to hinder the few doctors who are experimenting with the use of cannabis in the treatment of disturbed adolescents, amphetamine dependence, alcoholism and other conditions which are difficult medical problems. Although there have been few indications of success in this treatment, it is hoped that the new legislation will not interfere with these experiments.

In summary, the Wootton report found that most of the fears about cannabis were groundless. Physically it is much less dangerous than the other illegal drugs; most people can give it up readily and without withdrawal symptoms. Most cannabis users are industrious and law-abiding; there is no evidence that in Britain it provokes the user to crime other than the crime of possessing it. Nor is there any evidence to support the widely held belief that cannabis is a significant step in the escalation to heroin. It was agreed that cannabis is a potent drug, like alcohol, and that it was necessary to maintain restrictions on its availability for the time being; these restrictions would have to be more severe than they are for alcohol until more was known about the long-term effects of the drug. Nevertheless it was quite inappropriate to make cannabis subject to the same penalties as heroin under the Dangerous Drugs Act and it was wrong to send people to prison for the possession of a small amount. Research has been hampered and the law should be changed so as to encourage careful long-term investigations into the effects of smoking cannabis. When these results are available, the interim recommendations in the report should be reviewed.

These main conclusions were not so very different from the results found in earlier reports including the very thorough investigations made in India and the city of New York, and the more recent studies made in Canada and by the President's Commission in Washington. But the publication of the Wootton report was greeted with a chorus of abuse from politicians, press and the public.

8

Reactions to the Wootton Report

Prepublication Rumours

The last paragraphs of the report on cannabis were written in July 1968, but it was not published until January 1969. First it had to be read and discussed by the main committee. After some argument they agreed to endorse the report with a few amendments and an explanatory preface by the Chairman. It then had to be read by three Ministers, printed and published by HMSO. This gave plenty of time for rumours and leaks in the press.

There was an early guess in the *Sunday Times* in August reporting that the committee had 'run into serious difficulties attempting to find a realistic consensus', although the report had in fact been written by that time. In October several newspapers came out with the fairly predictable guess that the committee would reject the legalization of cannabis. Then on the 27 November the *Daily Mail* reported three specific recommendations of the committee; two of them turned out to be correct but one was wrong. That evening the *Evening Standard* gave the same story a full front-page spread, inviting comments from well-known people, as if the report had already been published. The next day all the daily papers reported the news, every one of them repeating the original mistake in the *Daily Mail*.

The *Daily Express* had a special article on the centre page as well as the inaccurate report on the news page; 'the most obvious argument against pot,' wrote James Wilkinson in this article, 'is that it leads to pot smokers mixing with hard drug addicts – those addicted to heroin and cocaine. And those who live off the weakness of others.' When the Wootton report was published, this argument was dismissed. The *Sun* devoted its main leader to comments on these guesses – surely the first time a newspaper has used its leading article to discuss an incorrect report about the unpublished recommendations of a Government committee. It repeated the escalation theory which was later discussed and rejected by the Wootton committee.

Quintin Hogg, the Shadow Home Secretary, talked of the need to 'pursue the addicts of hashish and marihuana with the utmost severity that the law allows'. Earlier at the Conservative Party Conference he had said that he was 'profoundly shocked' by the irresponsibility of those who wished to change the law. Mr Hogg said: 'I must frankly describe the arguments in favour of an alteration of the law in this respect as casuistic, confused, sophistical and immature. Of course we must make no mistake about this; it is all or nothing. There is no half-way house in this matter. There can be no encouraging the drug up to a point. You either sell it over the counter or in the shops or you prohibit it altogether.'

All this was happening long before the Wootton report was published. The Sunday papers continued with the news story and even weeklies like *New Society* commented on the original *Daily Mail* story as if it were a correct summary of the report. The disadvantage of a leak on such a large scale is that the general public really do believe that the report has been published. Not only do they get an inaccurate summary of the recommendations, but when the real report is published, there is a danger that it may be thought of as stale news. In fact even the journalists may be misled, for James Wilkinson in the *Daily Express* referred to a 'committee report just out' and the *Evening News* wrote about 'the Wootton report on drugs, just released', on the 28 November, forty-two days before the report was published. The effect of these leaks in the newspapers caused the resumption of the public discussion on cannabis, based on ignorance and prejudice, without the facts which the committee was set up to provide and which were the essential part of their report. The editor of a newspaper may think that he has got a marvellous scoop by jumping the gun, but he can hardly claim that his readers benefit from a premature and inaccurate report. And do the millions of readers of other newspapers realize or even care that they have been scooped?

It was also awkward for the Home Secretary and the other Ministers who were considering the report at the time these leaks occurred. In fact the views of the Home Secretary were also quoted extensively long before the report came out and he is supposed to have said on several occasions that he would require considerable convincing that a change in the existing law was desirable. Most of the papers gave the impression that Mr Callaghan was not likely to approach the Wootton report with an open mind.

With such a long interval between the completion of a report and the day of its publication, it is not difficult for newspapermen to find people who have seen a copy. In this case it is impossible to say where the leak started. The only clues are that all the news-papers repeated the mistake first printed in the *Daily Mail*. They all reported that the penalty for selling cannabis would be increased whereas the report recommended that it should be reduced. In addition *The Times* got the news that Peter Brodie, the Assistant Commissioner of the Metropolitan Police who was on the Wootton sub-committee, had dissented from one of the recom-mendations. In his minority report, Mr Brodie felt that the recom-mended penalty of two years for selling cannabis was too short.

Rejection

When the report was eventually published on 8 January 1969, most of the papers gave a summary of the report on other pages, but their front-page headlines emphasized its probable rejection by the Home Secretary.

> ROW LOOMS ON PLEA FOR POT   (*Daily Mirror*)
> STORM OVER POT SMOKERS CHARTER
>   (*Daily Express*)
> CLASH OVER SOFT LINE ON DRUG TAKING
>   (*Daily Mail*)

The front page of the *Daily Express* correctly reported the words of the report stating that there was no conclusive evidence that smoking cannabis led to heroin addiction. But the main article on

the middle page was headed: THE DEADLY PATH TO
ADDICTION. The discussion continued throughout the week
and into the Sunday papers where the comments ranged from
sensible to abusive. The *News of the World* front-page report was
headed: NOW THE DRUGS FLOOD IN. Their reporter
Simon Regan wrote: 'Foreign dealers flew into London the same
morning the Wootton report was published. In a matter of hours
the capital became one of the easiest places in Europe to buy
cannabis in the form of hashish concentrate.' Regan wrote that they
bought enough hashish to make 500 reefer cigarettes; it does not
seem to have occurred to him that he could have done this long
before the Wootton report was published. He gives the vendors of
cannabis credit for a degree of organization which is quite beyond
the capacities of the small operators.

Nearly all the popular daily and Sunday papers came out
against the report. Their indignant attitude is summed up by the
Daily Mirror editorial: 'In the middle of a growing drug problem
in this country a curiously permissive report has dropped on the
desk of the Home Secretary.' The more serious newspapers
rehearsed the arguments for and against retaining severe penalties
and only the *Daily Telegraph* was clearly in favour of all the
Wootton committee's recommendations. The weekly political
journals were equally uncertain. The *Spectator* thought the
'committee would have done better to have stayed its hand until
enough evidence was available to make an intelligent decision as to
whether or not the smoking of pot should be brought within the
law', while *New Society* felt the committee had been timid because
it had failed to recommend legalization which was the logical conclusion from the evidence it had reported.

An emotional attack on the report appeared as an editorial in the
British Medical Journal and the *Lancet* published a long leading
article in favour of the recommendations. Elizabeth Tylden, a
London psychiatrist, was quoted as saying 'this report is going to
cause the loss of young lives', but Dr Dale Cameron of the World
Health Organization said that while cannabis should remain
illegal, 'to apply penalties on the scale given to the possession or
use of narcotic drugs defies logic'.

Condemnation by the popular press and uncertainty in the opinion-forming sections of the community gave Mr Callaghan the chance to let it be known that the law relating to cannabis would not be relaxed as long as he was in charge at the Home Office. His immediate reaction appears to have been an attempt to sabotage any prospect of an intelligent and balanced debate on the Wootton committee's proposals. The usual procedure is to allow the report to be published, publicly discussed and eventually subjected to parliamentary debate without prior commitment by the Home Office. But on this occasion both the Home Secretary and his Shadow united in their condemnation of the report long before it was debated in Parliament.

The level of discussion during the debate in the House of Commons was quite surprisingly low.

When I talk to members of my profession and, often enough, to members of the medical profession, I find that, although they cannot always give figures which prove these facts, as has been the case all over the world, this drug is associated in their minds and professional experience with crime, violence and abnormality of one sort or another . . . (Quintin Hogg)

This mania for research that inspires sociologists and arm-chair legislators fills me with misgivings. There is a lot that we do not know about water, but I have a pretty shrewd conviction, at any rate when I am in a boat, that it is wet and better kept out and better not got into. (T. L. Iremonger)

The effects of cannabis are bad. It is all very well for the Hon. Member for Yarmouth to say that they are not bad. The essential of drug taking is that one has to take more and more to have the same effect. (Captain Walter Elliot)

I do not pretend to be an expert on this subject. The whole of our permissive society is so worrying that I would be prepared to leave the law, including the penalties under it, as they are. (Sir Douglas Glover)

The most colourful speech of all came from Mr Callaghan. He spoke of calling a halt to the rising tide of permissiveness; he called for more research but ignored the recommendation in the report that would make this research possible; he seemed to think the committee had recommended the legalization of cannabis ('My mind boggles about the thought of licensing the sale of cannabis by the local tobacconist, off licence, or whatever it may be,'); and he devoted more than half his speech to drugs with which the report was not concerned.

Most surprising of all, he said:

I think it came as a surprise, if not a shock, to most people, when that notorious advertisement appeared in *The Times* in 1967, to find that there is a lobby in favour of legalizing cannabis. The house should recognize that this lobby exists, and my reading of the report is that the Wootton sub-committee was over influenced by this lobby. I had the impression . . . that those who were in favour of legalizing pot were all the time pushing the other members of the committee back, so that eventually these remarkable conclusions emerged that it would be wrong to legalize it but that the penalties should be reduced.

In a letter to *The Times*, the Chairman of the Government Committee on Drugs and Lady Wootton wrote that Mr Callaghan's statement was 'offensive to our distinguished colleagues and ourselves'.

There was no doubt that the Home Secretary's treatment of the committee was discourteous and his remarks could hardly have been more insulting. In fact it was Mr Callaghan who had made up his mind before he had seen the report. If members of Government committees are going to be accused of being 'over influenced' and of being 'pushed back all the time', the others, by inference, are being accused of pushing back their fellows and resorting to doubtful tactics. Responsible members of the community can only be discouraged by the Home Secretary's unpleasant remarks from voluntarily sacrificing their valuable time to serve unpaid on these committees. In the words of an editorial in the *Guardian*: 'The Wootton committee produced a careful, authoritative report. It deserves better than the boorish brush-off it has received from the Home Secretary.'

But when all this has been said, there is no doubt that the public approved of the rejection of the Wootton report. Every public-opinion poll before and after the report was published has reaffirmed its belief that the severe penalties for the possession of

cannabis are necessary. The *Sun* reported that 'Labour and Tory
M Ps cheered Mr Callaghan when he announced that the cannabis
penalties would not be altered'. Only two Members of Parliament
had a good word to say for the report. A later debate in the House
of Lords was more sensible and responsible, but even here few of
the peers were prepared to accept the main recommendations of
the committee.

It is obvious that the Wootton report is quite unacceptable to the
general public. It is not easy to understand why the subject of
cannabis arouses such fears. It is equally difficult to explain how the
twelve members of the committee could possibly come up with
such an unacceptable result. None of them were young enough to
represent the under thirties. The committee was chosen by the
previous Home Secretary and included a distinguished social
scientist as its chairman, the Emeritus professor of psychiatry at
London University, the Tory founder and ex-editor of *New Society*,
several eminent medical men with experience of treating drug
users, a metropolitan stipendiary magistrate and a very senior
police officer.

It is possible that a description of the workings of this committee from the inside may help to explain public attitudes to
cannabis. I attended every meeting except one, and I will attempt
to explain how the committee reached its conclusions although
obviously I cannot name names or give away official secrets.

Inside the Sub-Committee

The sub-committee on cannabis under the chairmanship of Lady
Wootton was appointed in April 1967. At the first meeting a
month later there was some discussion about when we would be
ready to report to the main committee. The general feeling was that
we should be able to compile and write our report in time for a
meeting of the main committee in October of that year. But it took
us seventeen meetings and fifteen months before we could agree on
a final report.

At that first meeting I asked if we could initiate some original
research to supply information in some of the areas where this was

not available. Another member of the committee felt that this was not necessary and all we had to do was work out ways to stop 'the spread of this filthy habit'. It is incredible to look back at the hard and unsympathetic remarks made by several members of the committee at that first meeting and then to compare the reaction of the press when the report came out and see the members described as 'softies' and 'left-wing'.

At those early meetings there were six who wanted to take a tough line, four who were undecided, and two who felt the law against the possession of cannabis was too severe. After three meetings there seemed to be absolutely no common ground, but after ten meetings both sides had learnt from each other and were moving closer together. It was an interesting and rewarding experience to see the shift of opinion as the evidence was produced, sifted and studied.

As the weeks went by members read through the mass of material about cannabis. The secretariat must have sent us several million words to read. In addition there was written and oral evidence. Sixteen witnesses appeared before the committee ranging from pillars of the medical establishment to representatives of the pro-pot lobby. I was surprised by the ease with which most of them made assertions unembarrassed by the small amount of evidence to support their claims. On one occasion a witness revealed such ignorance on the subject that members of the committee were embarrassed. But on another occasion I tried to draw out a witness to give his views, but he was so incensed by the attitude of the committee that he decided to say as little as possible. One of the witnesses felt it was our duty to show how this evil could be stamped out, and another felt that we could not write a report on pot until we had all tried it at least once. I had some sympathy with the last view, but the enjoyment of cannabis is an acquired skill and I do not think any member of the committee had the opportunity to spend much time studying the effects of the drug at first hand.

Although the literature on cannabis is vast and the opinions of witnesses were numerous, it was difficult to get the necessary relevant information. When we asked for special material, it was sometimes found to be unavailable. The police were asked to supply a list of crimes in which cannabis had been a precipitating factor; a few weeks later a long list was produced from New Scotland Yard, but a study of the details of each of these crimes revealed that heroin, cocaine and usually amphetamines had been taken by the offenders, but none of them had used cannabis. That was in the days when one drug was much like another as far as the police were concerned.

In between meetings I and other members spent many hours studying the problem, not only reading all the material we could find, but going out of our way to talk to people in touch with the drug scene. In my case earlier researches gave me the opportunity to meet young people and obtain their views. I knew several people who smoked cannabis and I discussed the problem with them for hours on end.

A few members of the committee did not have time to study the subject in such depth. At some meetings it was obvious that one or two members had not read the relevant papers; sometimes they were to be seen reading a long report as others discussed it. But this was exceptional. For the most part members who had only a superficial knowledge of the subject when we first met became very well informed as the months went by.

A few officials from the Home Office worked full time with the committee and others from the Department of Health and the Scottish Home and Health Office attended all the meetings. These officials did not take a large part in the discussions (unlike the search and arrest sub-committee where the officials outnumbered and outspoke the members), but the chairman wisely brought them into the discussion when it was clear that their contributions would be useful.

Although they did not speak much, their influence was great because their job was to summarize and write up the discussion ready for the next meeting. When the discussions were long and rambling, it was often impossible to avoid bias when putting together the members' views in a form suitable for the official minutes. Perhaps it was not part of their job to avoid bias, for they were more aware than the committee members of what the Minister and senior officials would accept.

The quality of the officials' work was mixed. The earlier drafts of the report were abysmal. One official yawned so much at meetings that he made everyone else there feel sleepy. But for most of the time I was very impressed by the calibre to be found in the higher ranks of the civil service. Many of them had sharp quick minds. One of them, not mentioned in the obligatory paragraph of appreciation at the end of a Government report, clearly had a first-class analytical brain and gave invaluable assistance to the committee in the last vital stages of redrafting. Contrary to the usual image of civil servants, two members of the drugs branch at the Home Office were well known in the drug scene for their understanding and sympathy, and were able to win the friendship and trust of drug users despite their official position.

I had not previously had much experience of committee work, whereas others had and knew how to influence members to maximum effect. I would get exasperated and sometimes let my colleagues see it. One member was opinionated and dogmatic, and probably had little influence on the others. Another was well informed and argued cogently, but spoke too often so that other members got tired of his frequent interventions and took less notice of what he said. The rare interventions of another were always a valued contribution and impressed everyone. The most experienced committee worker was Lady Wootton who was also Madam Chairman. This put her in a position of great influence, but at every meeting she made sure that every point of view was heard. In certain paragraphs of the report her imprint is clear, but it is not true that she dominated the committee from the start. Indeed her own views changed and developed throughout the seventeen meetings, as did all of ours.

From the tenth meeting onwards we had all come to accept that cannabis was not at all like the other recreational drugs and required special consideration. In the debate in the House of Commons after the report was published, the Home Secretary criticized this point of view. He said that 'it was wrong of the committee to take one drug, look at it in isolation from the whole complex and background, and bring forward recommendations in the way it did'. But the Government Advisory Committee was given the task of reviewing the regulations covering all the recreational drugs. Unless we were to assume that there is no difference between one drug and another, it is hard to see how we could have proceeded unless we examined the particular regulations governing each specific drug. But in the cannabis report we did devote a whole section of ten paragraphs comparing cannabis with the other drugs.

By the thirteenth meeting we had arrived at our central conclusion, that it was inappropriate to bracket cannabis with lethal drugs, such as heroin, in the Dangerous Drugs Act. It became clear that the whole logic of our report demanded that there must be separate penalties for possessing cannabis. One member suggested that the difference could be shown by increasing the penalties for possessing heroin, but everyone else felt the penalties for possessing cannabis should be reduced. But by how much? The discussion was beginning to seem more like a heated argument when the Chairman intervened and told us that if we were ever going to get a reasonable report, everyone must be prepared to make some kind of compromise. This seemed to me to be a very proper intervention because we were getting near the stage where any attempt to reconcile opposing views would involve a loss of face.

Eventually eight agreed to the penalties as later published; two felt they were not severe enough, and two more felt they were too severe. After more discussion, both of the so-called hard liners were persuaded to go in with the majority. One of the so-called softies agreed with me and still felt the penalties were too high, but he also felt that unanimity was even more important. He talked to me privately and produced strong historical evidence to show that minority reports rarely had any influence and the impact of reports which were not unanimous were often seriously weakened. I was impressed by this argument and reluctantly agreed to a compromise which would in effect have altered the seventh recommendation so that there was no imprisonment for a summary conviction. But the other ten would not agree to this, stressing the value of a four-month sentence because this would allow the defendant to opt for trial by jury – a civil liberty most of us would be prepared to sacrifice if it meant risking a prison sentence. My ally felt that unanimity was more important and so I was left on my own.

Some people make a virtue out of obstinacy ('As I always say . . .') and are proud that their views never change. I had been most impressed by the way other members had considered the evidence and allowed themselves to be persuaded. The fact that eleven members of the committee with such diverse views at the beginning had now managed to reach agreement was much to their credit. I was not proud that I was the only one who had failed to come all the way to agreement. This was the first important committee to which I had been appointed and I felt that my inability to compromise indicated a lack of understanding and tolerance. Very few of the newspapers mentioned my reservations and it seems probable that they will have no effect for good or evil.

It was not the heavier penalties suggested by the majority of my colleagues that persuaded me to stick to my guns. The other members believed that the publication of the report would influence the behaviour of the police and the discretion of the judiciary. In fact they have been proved wrong because the rejection of the report by the Home Secretary has prevented it from having this effect. Young people are still being given prison sentences for having small amounts of cannabis in their possession.

In my reservation I wrote:

Nothing emphasizes the generation gap more than a drug offence. The drug user and the magistrate are basically out of sympathy. The cannabis user is partaking in a form of enjoyment – that is how he looks at it – which was unknown to the magistrate when he was young. In addition to this the clothes, hair style and attitudes of many young drug takers are unlikely to please the magistrate. Even if we adults feel inclined to put our trust in the magistrate's ability to understand these differences in the generations, it is quite certain that most of the young people of this country do not believe this wide gap can be bridged except by a very few. Why should they have to take their chance whether they get an informed and understanding magistrate or not? The administration of the law should not be a matter of luck.

Consequently I argued for a more sophisticated law in which the

T–D

seriousness of an offence is measured by the quantity in the offender's possession. If the offender has 30 grams or less in his possession, it should be considered a minor offence. Possession of larger amounts should rate higher penalties. I also felt that the blanket police powers to search anyone on the least suspicion were too far reaching; it may be possible to justify them for use against the more dangerous drugs, but not against cannabis which, the committee reported, is not harmful when taken in moderation.

As things turned out I was not to be the only dissenter. At practically the last meeting Peter Brodie, the Assistant Commissioner of Police, said that he felt that the big-scale trafficker would not be deterred by a large fine and the threat of two years' imprisonment. He proposed a five-year sentence in addition to an unlimited fine. This earned him a pat on the back from the many people who feel that the only solution to the drug problem is to stamp it out. Most of these people failed to notice that even Mr Brodie's recommendation was a considerable reduction in severity, from ten years, as the law was, to five. But the Home Secretary decided to increase the maximum penalty to fourteen years instead of reducing it by half as suggested by one of his senior policemen.

I have told the story of the way views were formulated inside the Wootton committee because it helps to explain why these people produced a report so unsympathetic to most readers. First of all, one must accept that the inevitable result must be a compromise when people with such very different backgrounds attempt to reach a conclusion. This is unsatisfactory in some ways, but not insensitive. Some people said that if there is not enough evidence, as the report admits, then it is illogical to recommend a change in the law. It may be illogical, but it is humane. It really does not make sense to send someone to prison for possessing a drug which is a mild intoxicant.

Others have said that it was a pity that Lady Wootton and her colleagues did not have the courage of their own arguments and recommend the legalization of cannabis. Despite the disappointment of the law reformers and the complete rejection by the general public, it is fair to say that the report was a rational reflection of the available evidence. Furthermore it was very nearly unanimous.

Mr Brodie only objected to one paragraph. I agreed with 92 of the 102 paragraphs. Such compromises as there were tended to be on language rather than basic principles. For example, in paragraph 70, some of us wanted to state clearly that cannabis psychosis, if it occurred at all, must be exceedingly rare in Western countries. Eventually we agreed on: 'Psychosis or psychological dependence, it is true, do not seem to be frequent consequences of cannabis smoking.' The committee often preferred the safety of a negative sentence when I felt a clear statement was required. I was particularly keen that misunderstandings about escalation to heroin should be clearly and finally resolved. Unfortunately the paragraphs in the report on escalation (48–51) do not seem to have had this effect.

The real conclusion about the Wootton report is that it would have been impossible to come to any other conclusion. I am quite sure that if the same evidence had been put before an equally varied group of citizens, they would have made similar recommendations if they had been allowed to study the subject long enough to overcome their unsympathetic attitudes to the use of any recreational drug.

This is the crux of the matter. The literature on cannabis is lengthy and confusing. Much of it is irrelevant; some of it is misleading; some of it is so interwoven with moral prejudices that true objectivity is lost. Until one has had time to go through this, sifting and sorting the valid information from the personal bias, it is inevitable that one will be misled by the prevailing myths. And yet the extraordinary thing is that nearly all those who have had the chance to go through the literature in detail have come to the same conclusions. This is true of two recent commissions in the United States (1962, 1967), of the Canadian Commission of Inquiry into the Non-Medical Use of Drugs (1970), and of the many individuals who, like myself, do not use cannabis and have no particular axe to grind.

9

The Escalation Theory

The Logical Fallacy

'It cannot be too strongly emphasized that the smoking of the marijuana cigarette is a dangerous first step on the road which usually leads to enslavement by heroin.' This is a quotation from a pamphlet issued by the United States Bureau of Narcotics in 1965. The most repeated argument against cannabis is that those who use it are likely to go on to more dangerous drugs, in particular heroin.

This is variously described as progression, predisposition, escalation and the stepping-stone theory. Here I shall use the word *escalation* because it has come into recent popular use to signify the deterioration of a situation.[1] Whichever word is used, the notion of cause and effect is implied – that cannabis *leads to* heroin addiction; or, to put it the other way round, a large number of people would have escaped heroin addiction but for their use of cannabis.

The Wootton report dealt with this controversy in four carefully worded paragraphs (48–51) and came to the conclusion that the 'risk of progression to heroin from cannabis is not a reason for retaining control over this drug'. This conclusion was reached after considerable discussion and the exhaustive examination of the available evidence, but it seems to have had very little effect. Both the press and public continue to make statements as if the Wootton report had never been written. The editorial in the *Daily Express* repeated the escalation theory as the reason for rejecting the

1. Whereas the word *progression*, used in the Wootton report, tends to imply improvement as well as forward movement.

report on the day it was published. A letter in the *Sunday Times* on 19 January 1969 asked: 'What about the more important information from people who have nursed many drug addicts whom they know have "graduated" from cannabis to heroin.' There have been many paragraphs in local papers similar to one that appeared in the *Hampstead and Highgate Express* on 22 August 1969, reporting a case of a twenty-year-old man found in possession of cannabis: 'The Chairman of the magistrates, Councillor Geoffrey Finsberg, said: "The bench is determined to stop this nonsense which leads on to harder drugs." '

Most people rule out the possibility of a pharmacological action which would predispose pot smokers to heroin. The most usual statement given in support of escalation is that most heroin addicts started on pot. The usual figure given is between 80 and 90 per cent and this is supported by retrospective investigations into the background of addicts, mostly from America. The same investigations show that the use of the word 'started' is misleading, because cannabis was by no means always the first drug the addicts had taken; nearly all of them had taken alcohol and tobacco before cannabis, and many had also taken amphetamines. The implication of the statement is that cannabis leads to heroin, but it is a logical fallacy to state that pot smokers will go on to hard drugs because the majority of heroin addicts have taken cannabis. One might as well say that most whisky drinkers will go on to methylated spirits because most meths drinkers have drunk whisky.

For many years investigators have studied the background case histories of drug addicts in clinics, hospitals and prisons. They can quite honestly and sincerely state that most heroin addicts have used cannabis. But this is not a statement of cause and effect. It is merely a statement of association. The statement immediately becomes false if someone interprets this sequence in time as a causal relationship.

It is also worth remembering that the relationship between heroin addicts and doctors at the treatment centres is a very special one. The addict is fully engaged upon the business of persuading the doctor to give him all the heroin he wants. The doctor is trying to cut down the daily dose. It is well known that junkies become expert liars and will say almost anything if it will help to wheedle a little extra out of the doctor. A junkie talking to a doctor who is known to be an advocate of the escalation theory is going to do his best to please him and would quickly agree to the implied suggestion that pot was the start of his downfall.

Evidence obtained from retrospective investigations into the previous habits of heroin addicts can never provide conclusive evidence to support the escalation theory. The only way to get a proper idea of the extent of escalation is to find a representative group of pot smokers and follow up their progress each year, noting how many go on to heroin, and how many continue to smoke only pot, and how many give up cannabis altogether. Such a research would take rather a long time and it would have to be a large group because even the most positive advocates of escalation do not put the number likely to go on to hard drugs higher than 15 per cent. Nevertheless it is surprising that no one has undertaken this research, considering the importance of the subject and the strong feelings that it arouses.

Correlation or Causality

Another important argument in support of escalation is that official figures show a sudden rise in arrests in 1957 followed by a rise in the number of heroin addicts two years later. Since then the number of addicts and cannabis offenders have continued to rise at about the same rate.

A considerable disadvantage of this evidence is that the figures are concerned with individuals who have been arrested or who are under treatment. As we now know, people who have come to the notice of police or doctors are hardly ever typical of a particular group of deviants. The same error was made about homosexuals. For many years the only research made into this phenomenon was by questioning homosexuals in prisons and clinics. But most homosexuals do not get arrested and do not seek treatment. It was not until a detailed study had been made of the attitudes and acti-vities of homosexuals who had not been in trouble that the real characteristics of homosexuality were better understood.[2]

It is equally misleading to make generalizations about all users of cannabis from investigations limited to studies of pot smokers who have been arrested or are under treatment – whether they have escalated to heroin or not. There is no doubt that there are certain types of pot smokers who are more likely than others to get arrested, perhaps because of their behaviour, clothes, colour, or simply because they make themselves more conspicuous. But most users of cannabis do not attract the attention of doctors or police.

It is dangerous to imply cause and effect because two phenomena have a high statistical association. It is not always possible to decide which is the cause and which is the effect. It would be possible to use the same figures to suggest that cannabis delayed the onset of heroin addiction – the 80–90 per cent addicts who have previously used cannabis might have become addicted to heroin one or two years earlier if they had not taken cannabis. A much more probable explanation is that both phenomena are caused by a third factor. In this case it may be an attitude of mind which includes the desire for recreational drugs. This would explain the association of cannabis with heroin addiction, not because one was the cause of the other, but because both are caused by the same trait – the desire for recreational drugs.

Certainly we need evidence of a different kind before we can deduce that cannabis leads to heroin *because* most addicts have used pot. In fact much of the evidence points in the opposite direction. If the escalation theory were true, there would be a more even distribution of heroin addicts throughout the country; over three quarters of all heroin addicts known to the Home Office live in London, but cannabis is smoked in many other areas. One would also expect more of the addicts to come from Pakistan or the West Indies; less than 3 per cent of all addicts on the Home Office list are coloured immigrants, but the Wootton report contained figures which showed that 38 per cent of all cannabis offenders were coloured.

John Kaplan (1970) has made a careful study of the overall

2. *The Sociological Aspects of Homosexuality*, by Michael Schofield. Longmans, 1965.

arrest figures in America and has come to the conclusion that 'if the stepping-stone effect exists at all, it will most likely be found only in certain particular segments of our society such as among poor Negroes and Mexican-Americans'. He compared cannabis offenders with heroin offenders and failed to find the same correlation that Paton (1968) and others have found here. Between 1960 and 1968 arrests in California for cannabis offences rose by 703 per cent, but arrests for heroin rose only 7 per cent; in 1960 arrests for heroin crimes were 52 per cent of the total adult drug arrests; by 1968 the percentage had fallen to 12 per cent.[3]

It is, of course, a much more meaningful comparison when both groups are offenders, but it is not possible to do this here because the number of people arrested for heroin offences is so small. In Great Britain the registered heroin addict does not need to buy his drug as he can get it free on prescription from a treatment centre. The situation in this country is in some ways ironic, for the pot smoker has to buy his supply, while the heroin addict can obtain his much more dangerous drug free if he registers at a treatment centre. I suppose this could be a possible reason why a pot smoker goes on to heroin although I have never heard anyone suggest this.

Statistical Calculations

The Home Office believes that most addicts have now registered, as it is obviously in their interest to do so. The largest group who have not registered would be the new addicts who have to admit to themselves that they are dependent on the drug before they can persuade themselves to go to a treatment centre to register. The result is that the total number of narcotic addicts in the country is known[4] to within a margin of error of two or three hundred.

We have no idea of the number of people who take cannabis. The Wootton committee felt unable to make any kind of estimate; they reported that guesses ranged between 30,000 and 300,000. This is such a wide range that it is not really possible to make sensible use of these figures. Furthermore I do not think a more accurate

3. Figures from the Bureau of Criminal Statistics, Department of Justice, State of California, 1968.
4. 1,466 in 1969.

estimate is possible at the present state of our knowledge.[5] In any case it is necessary to define what is meant by users of cannabis. Goode (1969) concludes that most of those who have tried cannabis do not use it more than a dozen times. If this is true, obviously it is important to distinguish between people who have tried it a few times and those who use it regularly. There is also a very large intermediate group who smoke pot intermittently and on rare occasions at parties or while away from home.

It is the total lack of knowledge about the number of cannabis users in Great Britain that undermines the arguments put forward by W. D. M. Paton (1968), professor of pharmacology at Oxford University, who is the best-known advocate of the escalation theory. He has compared the number of cannabis offences and the number of heroin addicts. In his graph, reproduced overleaf, the data is plotted with logarithmic ordinates so that rates of growth can be compared.

This figure reveals a strong association, but there are three things (already noted) to take into account.

1. Professor Paton is comparing two very dissimilar groups; one group is almost all the known heroin addicts, the second group is a small minority of cannabis users.

2. Cannabis users who have been arrested are not typical of the whole group.

3. A causal relationship should not be inferred from a statistical association without supporting evidence.

The major piece of evidence produced by Paton is based on the assumption (which hardly anyone would accept) that cannabis and heroin have nothing to do with each other; then he sets out to disprove this hypothesis. To no one's surprise, he succeeds.

The hypothesis is tested by using a method of inverse probability (a version of Bayes' theorem). By using this statistical manipulation, Paton calculates that 7–15 per cent of those who take

5. When the law is changed so as to permit research into cannabis, it will be possible to devise an inquiry, given sufficient time and money, to make a fairly accurate estimate of the incidence, just as it was possible to give reliable figures on teenage sexual activities a few years ago – *The Sexual Behaviour of Young People* published by Penguin Books in 1968.

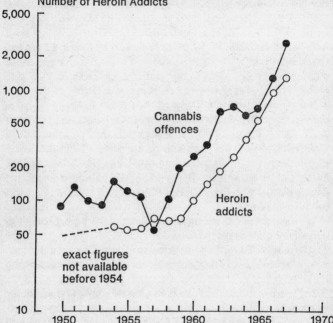

Comparison Between Cannabis Offences and
Number of Heroin Addicts

Cannabis offences

Heroin addicts

exact figures
not available
before 1954

cannabis will be, or are, heroin addicts.[6] He gets this result by
starting with a very low figure for the total number of cannabis
users. His estimate is far below the figures given in the Wootton
report. If he had taken the average of the two figures suggested in

6. Bayes' theorem states that $A = \dfrac{B \times C}{D}$ where

A = the incidence of heroin taking among cannabis takers.
B = the incidence of cannabis taking among heroin takers.
C = the incidence of heroin taking among the population at large.
D = the incidence of cannabis taking among the population at large.
Paton estimates that 90 per cent of heroin addicts have taken cannabis (B),
5 per 100,000 of the population take heroin (C), and 30–60 per 100,000 take
cannabis (D). By using these estimates, he calculates that A = 7–15 per cent
according to the value given to D.

this report (i.e. 165,000 instead of his figure of about 25,000), his result would have been far less than one per cent.

Paton concludes that 'there is, at least for our culture, a far closer connection between cannabis and the opiates than is generally realized'. This is an extraordinary statement when one considers that it is the general view that cannabis and hard drugs are closely connected, and it is the minority who feel that the escalation theory is based on spurious evidence.

Nor does Paton contribute anything of value by using a statistical manipulation[7] to disprove the statement that there is *no* connection between cannabis and heroin. No one in his right mind would insist that there is absolutely no connection between pot smoking and heroin use. It is the extent of the connection and its nature that is important. Most addicts have taken cannabis; the first experience of heroin is nearly always after taking pot, not before; cannabis consumption has risen in the last ten years and so has the rate of heroin addiction. All this is well known and not very surprising. One would expect to find some kind of connection between one recreational drug and another.

It is interesting that the escalation theory is always stated as a progression from cannabis to heroin, although the arguments would lead one to expect that it also applied to other recreational drugs. There is nothing particularly unique about the connection between cannabis and heroin. Paton's calculations show there is also a connection between amphetamines and heroin. Blum (1965) found that the correlation between opiate (including heroin) and cannabis use was no higher than that between opiate and amphetamine use, and it was lower than between opiates and sedatives, or tranquillizers, or glue, or nitrous oxide. On the other hand the correlation between cannabis and various other drugs was higher than with the opiates; for example, the correlation between cannabis and L S D was considerably higher than the correlation between cannabis and heroin. It seems likely that the escalation theory is just another way of making the unsurprising statement that people who have taken one recreational drug are more likely than non-users to have taken other drugs.

7. Bayes' theorem itself is the subject of controversy among statisticians.

Multiple-Drug Users

The most plausible explanation for the connection between cannabis and heroin is that among any group of illegal drug takers, there is a small minority who will turn out to be multiple-drugs users. These are disturbed individuals with severe personality disorders who will start on the drugs which are easiest to get, but will continue to try other drugs until they find one which they cannot discontinue in favour of another because they are trapped by its addictive power. The multiple-drug user is also particularly attracted by the ritual of injecting his drug intravenously. This was particularly noticeable after the epidemic of methedrine (an amphetamine) taken intravenously. When the supply was stopped the multiple-drug users turned to injecting a wide variety of other substances (including heroin, barbiturates and Mandrax).

The flaw in the escalation theory is that it postulates that there is something special about cannabis. Nearly all investigations show that most heroin addicts are multiple-drug users who have tried almost anything that has come their way. In Blum's (1965) sample of opiate users, 100 per cent drank alcohol, 95 per cent smoked tobacco, 78 per cent used cannabis, 73 per cent used barbiturates, 66 per cent amphetamines, 62 per cent tranquillizers, 50 per cent hallucinogens and 33 per cent other drugs. In James' (1969) study of addicts in prison, 88 per cent had used methedrine by injection, 75 per cent amphetamine tablets, 66 per cent had smoked cannabis and the same proportion had taken barbiturates.

Most multiple-drug users have the emotionally impoverished family backgrounds not infrequently found in other delinquent groups, such as high incidence of broken homes, poor school records, unemployment, work shyness, and police records. In the words of the Wootton report: 'It is the personality of the user, rather than the properties of the drug, that is likely to cause progression to other drugs.'

It is necessary to add that there is an element of infection. It is not possible to become a multiple-drug user unless one discovers how to obtain a multiplicity of drugs. It is unlikely that an individual, however severely disturbed, would become a multiple-drug user if he was born and remained in a remote village all his life. To this extent contact with other drug users in the hard drug scene is epidemic and fortuitous. Therefore the chance of a disturbed personality going on to heroin depends upon the setting in which he finds himself. There are areas and groups where cannabis use is extensive, but there is no problem of heroin addiction, for example, in Morocco; and there are areas and groups where heroin is widespread and cannabis is hardly used at all, for example, until recently in Vancouver.

People object to this concept because multiple-drug use is recent whereas individuals with personality disorders have always been with us. The answer is that if the disordered individual does not find his way to the drug scene, his disability will come out in some other way, perhaps more violent and disruptive. The disposition to multiple-drug taking involves complex psychological mechanisms which we are only just beginning to understand, but it is possible in the not too distant future that we may discover some characteristics which can help us to spot the potential drug abuser. Then in any group using recreational drugs it may be possible to predict that certain individuals will continue to experiment indiscriminately with dangerous drugs, and thus preventative measures may be devised.

The Distinctness of the Two Drugs

There are a few other arguments used to support the escalation theory. One is that tiring of the novelty or pleasure to be obtained from cannabis, users go on to other recreational drugs. The effects of pot are relatively benign and for some, it is suggested, this may not be enough. It cannot be guaranteed as a relief from depression. The novelist William Burroughs writes: 'It makes a bad situation worse. Depression becomes despair, anxiety panic . . .'

In fact most pot smokers look down on junkies and certainly do not feel that heroin has more to offer. Many regular users are very satisfied with the effects of pot and tend to reduce the dose as they become more experienced.

Heroin can not be described as a drug 'similar to cannabis, but stronger' – a description which some might use of LSD. Heroin is quite different. It is much harder for the experimenter to obtain, for, unlike pot, one has to have a working knowledge of the drug scene in order to buy heroin illegally. It is injected, whereas cannabis is smoked, and this involves an immense step emotionally for many people who are used to smoking but view the idea of using a syringe with abhorrence. Most important of all, the effects of the two drugs are so dissimilar; heroin is more like a sedative or a super tranquillizer. It is a drug that has attractions for the disenchanted who are constantly searching for something to provide escape from the tribulations of the real world. Cannabis increases awareness; heroin dulls the senses. Only rarely are both drugs attractive to the same person.

Another suggestion is that cannabis users must buy their supplies from the same source as the sellers of heroin: as both sources of supply are illegal, pot smokers have to contact people in criminal networks and run the risk of being contaminated. This argument fails on two counts. (1) Pot smokers rarely procure direct from big dealers, but buy from friends and fellow pot smokers. (2) Nearly all addicts get their heroin free on prescription. Consequently people who sell cannabis do not sell heroin.

This argument implies that it is the law and the police who are most responsible for the escalation from cannabis to heroin. Supporters of legalization say that it is the prohibition of cannabis, and not cannabis itself, which may lead on to heroin. There may be some substance in this. For many years teachers and others have been warning young people about the dangers of cannabis. Now that so many young people are discovering for themselves that it is nothing like so dangerous as they have been told, there is the risk that when they are offered heroin, they will not believe what they have been told about the dangers of hard drugs. Some who have been harassed by the police because they are pot smokers may decide that they will be no worse off if they go on to heroin. Indeed they will be better off so far as the law of the land is concerned, because they will be able to get their drug supplies legally; if they go to a treatment centre and register, they will get their heroin free. It is not possible to register with the Home Office as a cannabis addict.

Clark (1965), the American writer of a book entitled *Dark Ghetto*, argues:

The fact that those who use marijuana, a nonaddicting stimulant, are also required to see themselves as furtive criminals could in some part also account for the presumed tendency of the majority, if not all, drug addicts to start out by using marijuana. It is a reasonable hypothesis that the movement from nonaddicting drugs or stimulants to the addictive is made more natural because both are forced to belong to the same marginal, quasi-criminal culture.

The situation is different in America because all heroin is bought illegally and is expensive because supplies are controlled by the Mafia. No criminal syndicate thinks it is worth while to control marihuana in America or cannabis in Britain. The supplies come from too many areas and its users do not become continuous daily customers.

But it may well be true that outlawing cannabis has a deleterious effect. It encourages a disrespect for the law and forces the user to smoke in secret. Any minority group tends to adopt anti-social attitudes when it finds its activities are illegal. The effect is to 'criminalize' a large segment of our community and the result is bound to be disruptive.[8]

Nevertheless the majority of pot smokers do not associate with heroin addicts in spite of the fact that they are both using illegal drugs, and both have used, or still use, cannabis. The typical pot smoker has never met a junkie and has no access to heroin. Their way of life is distinct and their values are incompatible.

The Inevitable Conclusion

Some people believe that even if escalation operates in only a minority of cases, the needs of this minority are an overwhelming argument in favour of the prohibition of cannabis. At first sight this seems to be a question of numbers to be solved by adequate research. If it turned out that one in ten became addicts, most people would think the risk too great; if it were one in a hundred, many would still feel the chances were too high; if it were one in a

8. This important point is developed in more detail in chapter 12.

thousand, the argument would be less compelling. But the problem cannot be so easily solved. So long as cannabis is illegal, pot smokers as a group are going to contain an untypical proportion of rebels, drop-outs and people with personality problems. Even if it can be shown that one in a hundred of today's pot smokers will go on to heroin, it by no means follows that this proportion would be the same if cannabis were legalized.

The only reasonable conclusion is that escalation is best explained by the presence of potential multiple-drug users in any group taking an illegal drug. The Wootton report concluded that 'cannabis use does not lead to heroin addiction'. This finding is not unique. All the recent independent reports and investigations have come to the same conclusion. Bender (1963) writes that marihuana 'only occasionally is followed by heroin usage, probably in those who would have become heroin addicts as readily without marijuana' and Blumer (1967) reports: 'Popular conceptions of youthful drug use almost always presume that youthful users move along a line of development ending in heroin addiction. Our evidence offers no support to these conceptions but, instead, largely contradicts them.'

But there will still be many who remain unconvinced. It is almost as if the public wants to believe that those who smoke pot will end up as heroin addicts.

10

Crime and Violence

The Validity of the Evidence

The escalation theory is a comparatively recent controversy, but for very many years it has been alleged that the use of cannabis is associated with crime. This is particularly the case in America, where early records showed that at one time Commissioner Anslinger denied the possibility of cannabis escalating to heroin (Lindesmith, 1965) but he has always been sure that cannabis led to criminal activities. In an article headed 'Assassin of Youth', Anslinger (1937) found cannabis guilty of 'murders, suicides, robberies, criminal assaults, hold-ups, burglaries, and deeds of maniacal insanity . . . especially among the young'. In 1962 the White House Conference on Narcotic and Drug Abuse concluded that cannabis 'has received a disproportionate share of publicity as an inciter of violent crime', but the controversy still continues in America and, to a lesser extent, in this country.

The basis for this belief seems to be that the words *hashish* and *assassin* are derived from the same source, both named after a character known as Hasan-Ibn-Sabbath who lived in the eleventh century. He is said to have been the head of a fanatical tribe who thought up the idea of secretly murdering the leaders of enemy tribes instead of waging war. These murderers were known by the Arabic word *hashshashin* and his followers were said to be under the influence of hashish when they committed these atrocities.

It is, of course, ridiculous that modern social policy should be influenced by eleventh-century folklore, but the story is still quoted as a warning against cannabis. Indeed similar near-anecdotal evidence is often produced to support the association of crime with cannabis.

A near hysteria developed in America in the ten years before the war and this was reflected in reports in the British press. Sixty per cent of the crimes committed in New Orleans in 1936 were attributed to the use of cannabis and a Commissioner of Public Safety (Gomila, 1938) reported that 'youngsters known as "muggleheads" fortified themselves with the narcotic and proceeded to shoot down police, bank clerks, and casual bystanders'.

The most usual way of suggesting the connection between cannabis and crime is to produce long lists of potted case histories telling the story of a cruel offence committed by someone who is found to be a user of cannabis. Anslinger (1961) and Bloomquist (1968) have published lists like this, and Munch (1966) cites twenty-eight case histories. A typical example is the third case from Dr Bloomquist which describes a shooting incident and ends: 'When the female suspect was being booked, officers found two plastic bags containing marijuana in her purse.' This was the only mention of the drug and in most of these case histories no evidence is produced to show the individual was under the influence of the drug at the time of the crime.

Another frequent story is about a user of cannabis suddenly running amok, committing motiveless crimes of violence against innocent bystanders. Most of these case histories come from Eastern and Arabic countries where sudden fits of madness have been far from unknown long before they were attributed to drugs. Indeed motiveless killings are reported from time to time in America and this country without any suggestion that the deranged individual is taking drugs.

Sir Aubrey Lewis, in an Appendix of the Wootton report, gives several examples of chronic or excessive indulgence in cannabis leading to panic and violence. This is really no more than a collection of stories without the necessary documentation which would allow the reader to judge the extent that cannabis was an influence on the individual's behaviour.

For example, Sir Aubrey makes four references to the work of Dr Wolff (1949) in his Appendix. This is a book entitled *Marijuana in Latin America: The Threat It Constitutes* and Dr Wolff repeats many of the crime stories from other articles and books relating to

other countries far from South America. Kaplan (1970) has made
a careful analysis of this material and notes that Dr Wolff 'exhibits
what can be characterized only as a looseness in his handling of
facts'. In a highly emotional closing paragraph, Dr Wolff links
cannabis with insanity, crime, violence and brutality and refers to
it as, 'this weed, messenger of a false happiness, panderer to a
treacherous love . . . which makes him sick – morally more than
physically – and changes thousands of persons into nothing more
than human scum. It is this weed . . . of the brutal crime and the
burning hell . . . which sets free the spiritual and the bestial, and
makes the rabble bespatter pages with blood.' A writer with such
lack of detachment is out of place in an Appendix which aims to
review the clinical literature.

Later observers in South America (de Pinho, 1962; Moraes
Andrade, 1964) have contradicted Dr Wolff's results and found no
evidence that cannabis is an important cause of crime.

There are considerable difficulties in attempting to judge the
value of reports associating cannabis with crime. The first confusion is caused by the fact that it is a crime to possess the drug and to
sell it. The user found in possession automatically acquires a
criminal record. But it is necessary to distinguish between the
consequences of enforcing legal restrictions on drug users, and
the alleged criminogenic effects of smoking pot. Then there are the
same difficulties as those noted in the previous chapter on escalation, when a correlation is used to demonstrate cause and effect.

A further complication is that, in some countries at least,
cannabis is used extensively by those living in impoverished conditions. Among such people there is more than the usual amount of
delinquency. In certain communities it can be shown that a large
number of criminals use cannabis, but this does not necessarily mean
that the drug is a determining factor in the commission of crimes.
Bromberg (1934, 1939) showed that the number of criminals
who smoked pot was high, but in two large statistical studies he
found very little relation between crime and the use of cannabis.

In most of the case histories cited, the background of the
individual is unknown. A list of crimes committed by Mexican-
Americans who smoke pot is of little significance as they come

from a group where many use cannabis, whether they are criminals or not. Furthermore the published reports on individuals running amok only very rarely give a psychiatric history so that it is not possible to isolate the influence of the drug.

The same confusions arise as those noted in Chapter 3 when the effects of cannabis were discussed. Many of the reports of cannabis-induced crimes come from areas where opium, amphetamine or alcohol, are also being used extensively and it is impossible to tell which, if any, of these are to blame for the criminal behaviour. Likewise the potency of the drug varies from place to place and the amount the individual has taken is seldom stated in these reports.

Most surprising of all, it is usually hard to judge from these reports if the criminal has taken an overdose and so lost all control of himself; or if the criminal behaviour is induced by a chronic condition caused by taking cannabis regularly over a long period. In fact the history of drug taking, the amount and duration, is usually provided by the man himself, who often believes that it is in his own interest to exaggerate about the amount he has taken.

The Antithesis of Violence

It is strange that cannabis is usually said to be linked with violent crimes like murder, rape, and assault, and much less often with theft or other crimes where there are financial incentives. This is surprising because, of all the recreational drugs, cannabis is the one which induces lethargy and passive behaviour. On straightforward observation of the effects, it would seem to be the drug that is least likely to be connected with aggression.

Earlier (chapter 6) I have noted that cannabis is the apposite drug for the hippy culture with its emphasis on non-violence – 'the loving generation' and 'the flower children'. The rockers, skinheads, Hell's Angels and other aggressive teenage groups have found amphetamines much more to their liking. Many writers have made the point that cannabis is not likely to be the chosen drug of those who wish to indulge their aggressive instincts. Maurer and Vogel (1967) write: 'It has not been our impression from contact with many hundreds of marihuana users that these people are violent criminals; on the contrary, most of them appear to be rather indolent, ineffectual young men and women who are, on the whole, not very productive.' The Chopras (1942) write that excessive use of cannabis tends 'to make the individual timid, rather than to lead him to commit crimes of violence'.

Another fact that makes it hard to understand why cannabis should be connected with violence is the way the drug is usually taken. It is difficult to imagine the pot equivalent of a man gulping down a scotch to give him 'dutch courage'. Cannabis is a social drug which is nearly always taken in a group; there is usually a kind of ritual before lighting the joint and when passing it round; the company and the conversation is very much a part of the enjoyment. Incompatible company can spoil the effect for the drug takers (Matza, 1969).

But the influence of the group goes further than this; as Becker (1963) has pointed out, there is considerable interchange of folk knowledge about the effects, what to look out for and how to appreciate them. It is the quintessence of pot smoking to avoid agitation, never to lose one's cool. There is also a kind of protection afforded by the group. As smoking pot is illegal and therefore a secret activity, the group is likely to restrain anyone who gets 'stoned' or starts to do anything which creates a public display likely to attract the attention of the police. Drugs taken in group settings are much less likely to lead to violent behaviour than drugs like alcohol or amphetamines which are often taken in private.

Murphy (1963) writes: 'Most serious observers agree that cannabis does not, *per se*, induce aggressive or criminal activities, and that the reduction of work drive leads to a negative correlation with criminality rather than a positive one.' Many critics complain that the most serious objection to cannabis is that it creates a proneness to inertia and general passivity. It seems unlikely that the same drug can also lead to hostile and violent behaviour.

Five Possible Links

Although most of the case reports do not furnish sufficient material to allow us to make a sensible estimate of the possible link between crime and cannabis, five specific points deserve our attention.

(1) After taking cannabis for a long period, the user becomes demoralized.

(2) Criminals use cannabis to fortify them before committing a crime.

(3) Cannabis weakens inhibitions so that suppressed criminal tendencies arise.

(4) An overdose creates panic which leads to violence.

(5) Cannabis users are dangerous when driving cars.

Chronic use and demoralization. This situation is more likely to apply to other countries in which cannabis is taken in ghettos where there is already considerable poverty and crime. Cannabis is not the favoured drug of people in the poorest communities of Great Britain. It is true that users must find the money to buy the drug and they may choose to steal rather than work. But there is no sign of this being a major problem in this country at present and the evidence in other countries is confused because it is obtained from groups where crime is endemic. The general passivity of regular cannabis users makes it unlikely to be an important factor. Chronic pot smokers are not very interested in material possessions and they do not need much money; they are unlikely to resort to crime as long as they can obtain supplementary benefits.

Cannabis to fortify the criminal. The drug is not a stimulant and it is unlikely to be of much value to those who lack courage. A better suggestion is that pot is taken so as to have a calming effect on the nervous criminal. This is a possibility but it is also true that the drug would make him a less efficient criminal; the effect of cannabis may be that the crime is less expertly carried out and the offender is more likely to be caught. In some cases the use of pot may actually act as a deterrent; the user may lose interest and what once seemed a good idea may become too much bother. At any event cannabis does not have some mysterious power which forces people to perpetrate crimes which they would not otherwise commit.

Inhibitions are lowered. The evidence for this usually comes from the police and is often confused because the reports usually recount incidents which involve several drugs including alcohol. Until recently police officers tended to group all drugs together as equally likely to lower inhibitions. It may well be true that suppressed criminal tendencies may arise under the influence of cannabis, although it is probably more correct to state that the drug impairs judgement rather than lowers inhibitions. It is equally true of most other drugs; indeed the reason for taking a recreational drug is to achieve a subjective state not ordinarily available and a release from conventional restraints is clearly one of the great attractions of any recreational drug. But there is no doubt that alcohol is much more effective in lowering inhibitions against violence, and if this were the prime object of the drug taker, he would choose to drink rather than smoke pot. In fact cannabis tends to accentuate all traits of the personality, both harmful and beneficial.

Panic through overdose. The Wootton committee reported that even the severest critics of cannabis did not regard it as the direct cause of serious crime in Great Britain. But influenced by Sir Aubrey Lewis' catalogue of anecdotes, they did allow that an excessive dose might lead to agitation, excitement or panic. There really is very little evidence to support these claims. There are no reports of such events which have occurred in Great Britain and Becker (1967) in a special study of the medical literature could only find three papers on this phenomenon. The reports from other countries (Keeler, 1967; Jorgensen, 1968; Milman, 1969) suggest that predisposition to panic is always present and there is usually a long psychiatric history. Even Bloomquist[1] who testified before a Senate Committee that toxic proportions of cannabis could cause 'heinous crimes due to paranoia, megalomania with increased strength, lack of socio-moral inhibitions and release of basic destructive trends', wrote in his own book (Bloomquist, 1968): 'Because of the relative mildness of Mexican and American varieties of cannabis we have seen very little of cannabis-induced

1. Testimony before California Senate Public Health and Safety Committee, 18 October 1967.

reaction. But with the coming of more potent oriental varieties, with the coming of hashish, we can look for more and more instances of psychosis and violence as a result of cannabis use.' But this prediction is not confirmed by experience in Great Britain where the resin (hashish) is more often smoked than the leaves (marihuana).

The number of psychotic reactions to cannabis are far rarer than one might reasonably expect. In a drug-orientated society it would seem quite natural to turn to the drug of one's choice (usually alcohol) when faced with a stress situation. But the potency of cannabis is usually so low that it is not really all that easy to take an overdose, as it is with other drugs like alcohol, amphetamines, barbiturates. Furthermore the reaction to cannabis is so quick that it is easier to control the effect and so avoid taking too much by mistake. It should be remembered that the fatal dose of cannabis in man is unknown because no reliable account of such an event has ever been reported (Goodman and Gilman, 1965).

Cannabis and driving. In his review of the clinical literature, Sir Aubrey Lewis reported: 'The one delinquency which receives general reprobation is driving while under the influence of cannabis.' Even the report from the National Council for Civil Liberties (1969) notes: 'As cannabis can cause distortion of perception and a decrease in reaction time, it would be dangerous to drive under the influence of this drug.' But recent researches have cast some doubts upon the magnitude of this. An experimental study from the State of Washington Department of Motor Vehicles (Crancer, 1969) has shown that cannabis has very little effect on driving ability. Weil (1968) found that the performance of novice users of cannabis deteriorated slightly in tests of physical and mental dexterity, but sophisticated pot smokers actually improved their performance in these tests. This is in line with the saying in cannabis circles that inexperienced users find it difficult to drive while high, but regular users have no difficulty. Joe Rogaly, writing in the *Financial Times* about a group of young Americans he met at Cape Kennedy, had surprising confidence in them. 'My wife quickly decided it was safe to let our young children drive in their van with them, even though they were high on marijuana. For the effect of this drug on these young people seemed to give them an all-pervading gentleness.' It is obvious that much more research is needed because the information now available shows that the situation is not as definite as was once thought.

The Attitudes of Police and Criminals

The strongest advocates of the idea that cannabis leads to crime are the police, and as they are the group who most often meet criminals, their advocacy deserves some attention. The problem is similar to the logical fallacy encountered with escalation. The police believe that many criminals use cannabis and therefore those who take this drug are likely to commit crimes.

In fact there is some doubt whether it really is true for this country that many criminals smoke pot. It is much more likely to be true in the ghettos of Arabic countries and in the urban slums of America where the rates for delinquency and cannabis use both tend to be high. In a group where pot smoking is fairly common, it is likely to be the more aggressive types who are the first to try the drug in much the same way that it is the bold ones who start to smoke and drink at an earlier age – the boys who never refuse a dare for fear of being called 'chicken'. But these types are not often regular pot smokers because they find alcohol is more suited to their aggressive instincts.

The police are concerned about enforcing all the laws and the distinction made in this chapter between the crime of possessing cannabis, and other criminal acts while under the influence of the drug, is a nicety that does not interest them very much. They are out to prevent all crimes and to stop the use of all recreational drugs. Consequently they are apt to think of one drug as being as bad as another. They know that alcohol and amphetamines (Scott and Wilcox, 1965; Hart and Nation, 1966) are used by many criminals. They do not feel disposed to make an exception in the case of cannabis. In fact cannabis, unlike alcohol or amphetamines, cannot as yet be detected in the body, so the evidence depends upon finding a quantity at or near the scene of the crime, and upon statements made by the accused.

Offenders often think it will be to their advantage to base their defence on alleged intoxication by cannabis, and information about the amount of the drug taken is usually provided exclusively by the man himself, who may believe that it is in his own interest to exaggerate. Just as the accused sometimes pleads decreased responsibility because he was drunk, another man will claim that cannabis provoked his criminal behaviour which he cannot now recall and for which he cannot be held fully responsible.

Although this claim is sometimes made, the truth is that cannabis will not produce a 'black-out' similar to the loss of memory under the influence of alcohol. It is difficult to believe the reports about individuals who have taken so much cannabis that they do not remember what they have done. People under the influence of cannabis may act unconventionally and anti-socially, but they know what they are doing and cannot escape responsibility for their behaviour.

There is no doubt that criminal acts are committed while under the influence of cannabis, but the reports have exaggerated the numbers and the extent of this influence, and it is clear that cannabis is nothing like so criminogenic as alcohol, the most commonly used drug in our society. The reasonable conclusion is that abuse of cannabis should be subject to legal control just as abuse of alcohol is similarly controlled. Lawrence Kolb (1962) reviewed five careful studies by competent investigators in America and found no association between cannabis and aggressive crime, nor was there any evidence that such a thing as a cannabis-induced murder had ever occurred. This conclusion is supported by animal experiments (Garattini, 1965) which showed that the pharmacological effects of cannabis tended to inhibit aggressive instincts.

Foreign reports that connect cannabis with crime are not persuasive and there are no British reports of this kind. It is clear that cannabis has little effect on the behaviour of the criminal, or on the number of the crimes. Criminals may use the drug but it is not a determining factor in the commission of crime.

Conflicting Reports

For many years cannabis has been associated with sensuousness, carnality, debauchery and sexual gratification. Many of the reports in the press have made their exposures of drug taking sound positively pornographic, suggesting that an evening which begins with cannabis is likely to end with a sexual orgy.

The press stories are probably inspired by the sex-loaded campaign against cannabis carried on by Anslinger. In 1953, he wrote: 'In the earliest stages of intoxication the will power is destroyed and inhibitions and restraints are released; the moral barricades are broken down and often debauchery and sexuality result.' Anslinger also wrote an introduction to Wolff's book, *Marijuana in Latin America: The Threat It Constitutes* in which sexual orgies are reported as the frequent consequence of taking cannabis. Ausubel (1964) writes that 'exhibitions of perverted sexual practices ("circuses") are not an uncommon feature'. In a recent court ruling the Chief Justice of the Superior Court of Massachusetts held that sexual promiscuity was one of the undesirable consequences of marihuana use.

Kaplan (1970) noted an interesting case which shows how sex is apt to creep in even when it is not in the original document. Donald Miller, General Counsel of the US Bureau of Narcotics, summarized the work of Professor C. G. Gardikas in a talk to the National Student Association. Miller (1967) said that in the Greek professor's group of hashish-smoking criminals, 117 men 'had between them more than 420 sentences for assaults, woundings, threats, robberies, manslaughter and sex offences'. In the original report Gardikas (1950) disavows any link between cannabis and sex offences.

Most of the leading authorities would agree with this. The Indian Hemp Commission reported that cannabis did not lead to sexual misconduct. The Mayor of New York's Committee on Marihuana reported that the drug did not stimulate sexual desires. The White House Commission states: 'Although marihuana has long held the reputation of inciting individuals to commit sexual offences and other anti-social acts, evidence is inadequate to substantiate this.'

Supporters and opponents of cannabis law reform tend to agree that the drug does not stimulate sexual desire. Professor Lindesmith (1965), a persistent critic of the Federal Bureau of Narcotics, writes: 'Among those who have never used hemp or seen it used by others the belief is often found that marihuana acts as a sexual stimulant or aphrodisiac. Actually its effects, like those of opiates, are exactly in the opposite direction, tending to cause the user to lose interest in the opposite sex.' Constantinos Miras (1969), one of the drug's severest critics, reported that cannabis actually impairs sexuality and that when given to rats their rate of 'reproduction activity' declined 90 per cent. Hart and Nation (1966), in their study of girls in a remand home, reported that those who smoked cannabis 'are seldom promiscuous'. Dale Beckett (1967) writes: 'Like alcohol, cannabis increases the desire but takes away the performance. The fascinating images of sex orgies at teenage pot parties are just images.'

Sexual Desire

Many users have reported erotic ideas or sensations but have not felt inclined to give active expression to them when under the influence of the drug. Some users, but by no means all, would agree with Théophile Gautier (1846) when he declared: 'Romeo as a hashisheen would have forgotten his Juliet.' Others would prefer the account by the novelist Alexander Trocchi:

Experts agree that marihuana has no aphrodisiac effect, and in this, as in a large percentage of their judgements, they are entirely wrong. If one is sexually bent, if it occurs to one that it would be pleasant to make love, the judicious use of the drug will stimulate the desire and heighten the pleasure immeasurably, for it is perhaps the principal effect of marihuana to take one more intensely into whatever the experience. . . . It provokes a more sensual (or aesthetic) kind of concentration, a detailed articulation of minute areas, an ability to adopt play postures. What can be more relevant in the act of love?

Without necessarily agreeing with all that Trocchi says, it is possible to get a better understanding of the effects of the drug by separating sexual desire from sexual pleasure. It does appear that, for most people, cannabis will not stimulate desire and for many the effect will be blissful contentment with the present effect of the drug, so that sexual activities are of small interest. In an informal survey of 200 users, Goode (1969) found that more than a third said cannabis had no effect on their sexual desires, but 44 per cent replied that it increased their desires. A possible explanation is that it depends to a large extent on the situation; if the user is with someone with whom he is already intimate, pot acts as a stimulant; but if he is smoking with strangers, the prospect of sex becomes less desirable than ordinarily.

It is also quite possible that cannabis lessens inhibitions. There is an account of one man who indulged in frank exhibitionism during a trial study of volunteer subjects carried out for the New York report; it was later discovered that this man, who was not a regular user of cannabis, had been arrested on three occasions for indecent exposure. Two studies of cannabis use in the army concluded that it encouraged homosexual activities (Marcovitz, 1945; Charen, 1946).

It is not hard to believe that a man with suppressed homosexual desires might feel free to express them while under the influence of cannabis. On the other hand, Timothy Leary claims that Allen Ginsberg, a self-declared homosexual, had his first woman while under the influence of pot. Furthermore Chopra (1957) mentions that certain 'saintly people who wish to renounce world pleasures use cannabis drugs for suppressing sexual desires'.

Sexual Pleasure

There is some doubt about the effect of cannabis on sexual desire, but the information on sexual pleasure, though small, is less conflicting. Users have always maintained that pot increases tactile sensitivity and so love-making is more intense. Some men have claimed that it helps to prevent premature ejaculation. Goode (1969) found that frequent users were more likely to claim that cannabis increased sexual enjoyment.

It is very probable that experience is more important than the amount taken or the potency of the dose. Too much cannabis will merely make the user sleepy and then the only erotic experience he can have will be in his dreams. But an experienced pot smoker controls his high so that all feelings are enhanced. Listening to music, reviewing familiar scenes, even eating, may take on a new interest and awaken new sensations. The same enhancement would also increase sexual excitement.

Throughout history man has diligently sought a miraculous aphrodisiac, so far with very little success. In the old days people believed in the magical principle that like cures like. For example, heart-shaped leaves were believed to cure heart disease, and the horn of a rhinoceros was thought to be of benefit to a man who could not get an erection. Even today there is demand for rhinoceros horn, ground up into a powder and taken by mouth. Cannabis would be better than that because it relies less on 'sympathetic magic' and more on bringing about a change in the user's mental state. Many people have doubts about their sexual capacities and if the drug increases self-confidence, it may be helpful. But cannabis is unlikely to act as an aphrodisiac in the sense that it will restore or invigorate sexual power. Nor will an overdose lead to perversions, rape or violent sex. But if the pot smoker is sexually orientated, or finds himself in a sexual situation, then it is possible that his response will be more intense than if he had not been under the influence of the drug.

12

Pot Heads

The Extent of Use

Several of the witnesses who appeared before the Wootton committee said that they smoked cannabis[1]; and they were able to give useful information on different types of users. Although it was impossible to estimate the relative size of any of the groups they identified, it was clear that smoking pot had now spread from the original groups of immigrants, seamen and musicians to middle-class students and, more recently, to working-class youths. The proportion of coloured immigrants is probably not much higher than in the white indigenous population; the essential difference is that it is not thought to be a heinous crime in Pakistan or the West Indies to be found smoking pot. In all of these groups the extent of use varied from small to great. Although it is difficult to make arbitrary divisions, the most meaningful way of classifying pot smokers is according to the extent to which they use the drug – experimental, sporadic and regular.

At one end of this scale come the people who try it once or twice as an experiment. A very large number stop there and never again use cannabis. Perhaps the experience was unpleasant or, more likely, dull and unexciting; perhaps further opportunities did not arise or were not thought to be worth the risk. It is plainly absurd to think of these as pot smokers, yet some researchers ask their subjects if they have ever taken cannabis. Thus people whose only experience is three or four drags at a communal joint are included in the total number of cannabis users.

1. All witnesses were assured that their evidence would remain confidential and were given an indemnity against legal action as a result of anything disclosed.

Next in the continuum come the sporadic users who smoke on the rare occasions when they are with others using cannabis; for some this may be once a month, for others as little as once a year. It is possible to classify them all into one group because they make no effort to seek or possess cannabis; it is a pleasant, but dispensable and unimportant aspect of life.

These two groups of experimental and sporadic users are only important in two ways. At the time they are smoking they are just as vulnerable as any other user of an illegal drug; they may be arrested, imprisoned or given some other sentence with all the consequences of acquiring a criminal record, including a poor reputation and possible loss of employment. The second point is that the use of cannabis by these people is of no social concern, and is quite harmless, unless it can be shown that the experimental or sporadic user is likely to become a regular user.

There are two types of regular users. People in the first group smoke several times a week, perhaps at least once a day, but for most of their waking life they are not under the influence of the drug and are mixing with people who do not use cannabis. The others are the real pot heads, who are high almost all their waking hours. People who smoke as much as this will find that cannabis has become the central element in their lives. All their friends will use cannabis and they will want to be under the influence of the drug while working, resting, listening to music, having sexual intercourse or simply meditating; to be high will be their normal state.

These people used to be called pot heads, but the phrase has gradually been devalued by use in the vernacular and has lost its specific meaning, so that now any regular user of cannabis is called a *head*. The number of persons who are so completely involved in cannabis is very small. Goode (1969) estimates that extensive users are less than one per cent of all those who have ever tried cannabis. Dr Roger Smith, working in the Haight Ashbury clinic which ministered to what was probably the highest concentration of cannabis users ever known, told Kaplan (1970) that there were very few who took the drug in sufficient quantity to interfere with their functioning in the community.

Although the users have been classified into groups, individuals change in the extent of their use and move freely from one group to another – and the movement is not in one direction only. A sporadic user may increase his consumption, but equally a regular smoker may stop because it becomes risky to get further supplies or because other interests predominate.

Regular Users

Although extensive users of cannabis are very rare, it is under-standable that much concern is expressed about such prolonged and excessive use. In chapter 3 reference was made to foreign reports which suggested that long and heavy use of cannabis would lead to a general deterioration of the personality, but the evidence is not convincing. Other authorities (Allentuck, 1942; Freedman, 1946) maintain that even prolonged and obsessive use of cannabis does not lead to physical, mental or moral degradation. The Chopras (1957) write: 'Those who indulge in it habitually can carry on their ordinary vocations . . . and do not become a burden to society or even a social nuisance.'

The idea of cannabis psychosis arose because the early reports came from countries where cannabis was used by the very poor and deprived. It was the same kind of thinking that started the idea that masturbation led to insanity. People saw mental patients masturbating in mad houses, because they were bored or for a variety of other reasons, and they naïvely assumed that one was the cause of the other. The same primitive logic persuaded un-critical observers to assume that anyone who took cannabis would end up in the kind of degradation to be found in the slums of the Middle East. But a slum is no place to collect a representative sample. The personalities of slum dwellers who use cannabis are not useful indications of the personality characteristics of other users.

The suggestion that cannabis can lead to diminished initiative may be nearer the truth. The excessive user finds that the drug brings him most of the satisfactions that he needs. The ordinary problems that occur in everyday life are taken lightly and he is buoyed up by a cheerful optimism that things will work themselves out all in good time. It is an attitude of mind that would be of value to some of us who worry too much, but it could also mislead others with a lazy disposition into feeling that no effort is required to solve their various problems.

A more serious accusation is that the heavy user suffers from a general disorientation of purpose. Rosevear (1967) is a strong supporter of legalization, but he notes: 'Many who are under the drug's spell find that simple acts, such as getting a glass of water, are laborious, and it is not uncommon to find a person who is intoxicated so disorientated that he will be standing in the middle of the kitchen, glass in hand, wondering what on earth it was he was about to do.'

Regular smokers are sometimes known as 'losers'. They tend to lose interest in projects and are often unsuccessful in the ordinary, worldly aspects of life. They lack ambition for material success and so do not care much about financial stability or social approval. But the number of cannabis takers who become excessive users is so small that it seems likely that there is already a particular psychological trait in their personality. It is difficult to separate cause and effect in this situation, and it is not clear whether cannabis causes them to be unsuccessful, or whether their inability to fit into ordinary society causes them to take too much cannabis.

Another complaint about regular users is that their attitude is basically anti-intellectual. They tend to adopt the ideas of the underground youth (ex-hippy) movements and some of these notions do not go much further than a mindless search for the joys of love. Few pot heads read books and many are hopelessly inarticulate even when on campaigns of genuine social and moral worth.

For many music is a more vivid form of communication than words; pop music has now developed beyond its original commercial simplicity, but even at its best, it can arouse emotions but not logical thought processes. Pot heads are usually attracted to art and poetry which is concerned mainly with the incongruous and the absurd. They are more interested in the mood of a film or novel than in the plot. Most of all there is a strong preference for emotional reaction instead of chains of thought. People, like myself, whose writing and thinking depends upon 'linear' sequences of reasoning find it difficult to follow these bursts of insight. But our inability is the result of our training, which has limited our field of vision, and we must be careful not to be too critical of something we do not really understand.

A Secret Life

Cannabis is a social drug and is nearly always smoked in a group. There is no cannabis equivalent to the secret drinker, who hides a bottle in his or her room and develops a dependence on alcohol unknown to friends or family.

The beginner would find it quite difficult to smoke pot on his own. First, he must know someone in order to get a supply; even if he knew where to go, a dealer would hesitate to sell to a stranger. Then he needs to learn the special technique of smoking the drug so as to gain the maximum effect; few people get much pleasure from their first attempt to take cannabis and the novice must learn to perceive and appreciate the effects of the drug.

A group also provides valuable psychological support. Before a beginner smokes pot, he must overcome a powerful set of deterrents. He knows that it is illegal and the punishment will be severe if he is caught. He knows this behaviour can lead to social ostracism by people who are important to him – his family and friends. It is also likely that he has, to some degree, accepted the traditional views which look upon cannabis as a sign of moral degradation. He needs a demonstration that the drug is pleasurable and not harmful. In other words he must become an 'insider' before he can become a regular pot smoker.

The influence of the group can also be beneficial. The beginner learns to control the effects of the drug, so that he obtains euphoric sensations without becoming incapable or stoned. But the group also makes it easier for the sporadic user to become a regular smoker. At first the casual user smokes when it is available, which usually means when he is with others who have a supply; when this is not the case, he does not smoke. But after a series of chance encounters of this kind, he begins to feel under an obligation to contribute. So he asks someone else in the group where he can buy cannabis and he is taken to a dealer, who prefers a personal introduction as he may fear a police trap when selling to a newcomer. So the first supply is bought through the group, whose influence becomes still more binding.

Gradually he acquires a new set of friends and he probably feels that they have to be kept apart from his old friends, and so he is now leading two lives. Perhaps he is known as a respectable citizen to his business acquaintances who, if they knew he took cannabis, might regard him as an unfortunate dope fiend. Although the number of people using cannabis is increasing rapidly and this is bound to lead to more tolerance and better understanding, it is still true that the pot smoker is outside normal social boundaries for most people.

There are a large number of reasons why a young person will try to keep his pot smoking secret. First of all it is illegal and an otherwise law-abiding individual is often reluctant to commit a crime. He knows that if he is discovered by the police he will be subject to severe penalities, perhaps even a prison sentence. He may get into trouble even if he is not misbehaving or abusing the drug and he can be arrested even before he has started to smoke it. In addition to this, he may lose his job if his employer gets to hear about his drug taking. Unless they are unusually well informed, his friends and relatives will regard his use of cannabis as a sign of irresponsibility and lack of self-control.

It is not difficult to remember, because it is not long ago, my reactions when I first heard about a friend who took cannabis. I did not know much about recreational drugs and assumed, almost without thinking, that cannabis was in the same category as opium and other dangerous drugs. I tried to be tolerant but could not help regarding my friend with pity and concern. It never occurred to me at the time that it might be a conscious choice by a sensible man, who had thought carefully about the situation before deciding to take it.

The need to lead this double life produces a vague kind of paranoia in some individuals. He begins to suspect that he is being followed; he suddenly switches to another dealer because he fears a trap; he crosses to the other side of the street when he sees a policeman, even if he is not carrying cannabis at the time, because he fears that he will be stopped and have the drug planted on him while being searched; he thinks his telephone is being tapped and his home is being watched by the police; the ritual before smoking involves meticulous and excessive precautions. Of course this feeling of persecution is not always imaginary. The police will go to a great deal of trouble to catch drug takers and the basis for his fears may be real.

A double life of this kind will often involve lies, subterfuges and time-table manipulations, which in turn create tension and distrust between people who previously were friendly. Some people are so depressed by the need to keep their drug taking secret that they decide that it is not worth while. Others manage to keep their two lives apart, even when it means adopting two standards and complying with two different conventions. Still others resolve the dilemma by opting out of the normal world, choosing to live in a social group where cannabis is accepted.

Introverted Groups

A cannabis-orientated group has its own elaborate culture. Much of the talk is about pot. If the neophyte is to feel at ease with the others in the group, he must be table to talk knowledgeably about the different types of cannabis in the same way that a connoisseur talks about wine.

In such a group his life will centre around cannabis. He will be influenced by close friends, all of whom smoke pot. But this decision to join this group goes beyond the desire to smoke when he wants to. It is not just the drug which will monopolize his interests and absorb all his time. It is the different way of life which he will find so compelling.

He will now be in a group whose values and activities will be opposed to those of the larger conventional society. The people in such a group tend to think of themselves as a race apart – not only different, but in some way superior. The new member of the group will feel emancipated and free at last from the 'grey' people in the

materialistic world outside. He will be apathetic and uncommuni-
cative when work or family obligations take him away from his
cannabis-orientated world and he will spend every free moment
with others who share the same group attitudes. The pot culture
will dominate his whole life.

These groups are in no way anarchical. There are fairly strong
standards which exercise a powerful influence on behaviour. The
members share a group language and cultural interests; they accept a group norm of behaviour and hold similar attitudes towards
political and social institutions. There is a strong group ethic and
departure from these standards is viewed with the same disapproval
as unconventional behaviour is regarded in ordinary society.

In some groups the standards are high, but they all suffer from
the defect of exclusiveness. As their use of cannabis is illegal, there
is a strong sense of self-protection. Outsiders are discouraged and
it is a long time before newcomers are accepted into the circle, with
the result that the attitudes of the group, which are sometimes
biased or distorted, are less likely to be corrected. The absence
of outside streams of thought is restricting and unhealthy, and
leads to the development of introverted minority groups.

Cannabis Coteries

When society comes across a minority within itself, its first action
is to try to assimilate it. But if this is not possible, then the minority
suffers discrimination and the result will be the formation of introverted minority groups. Professor Allport (1954) in his book, *The
Nature of Prejudice*, has listed some of the traits which characterize
these groups, and similar characteristics have been noted by Little
(1947) among Negroes, Robb (1954) among Jews, and Westwood
(1960) among homosexuals. The cannabis coteries are no exception.

One trait, already noted in this chapter, is the anxiety and paranoia which is common to these introverted groups. Another is the
strengthening of ties within the group after rejection by the
dominant society. Another characteristic is the tendency to quarrel
among themselves (e.g. the disputes on the editorial boards of *IT*

and *Rolling Stone*), but to band together against outside authorities. Another trait, found particularly in religious minorities, is the attempt to be self-sufficient by setting up small rural communities, as many of the cannabis groups have done in the United States. In urban society, influential members of the group give employment or other important positions to people in the same group. Another characteristic is for such groups to become more formalized, with their own organizations and periodicals, taking as their aim the protection of their civil liberties against the prejudices of the dominant majority; Release and Bit are examples of this in the cannabis underground. It is clear that many of the characteristics of the cannabis coteries are common to all introverted minority groups and share many of their disadvantages.

Non-Conformists

Although introverted groups can be disruptive, it is important to emphasize that this is not an objection to minorities as such, or to individuals who do not conform. A man who is forbidden by fear of exposure, trial and punishment from carrying on an activity which he is convinced is harmless to others and to himself is likely to take a cynical look at some of the other customs and standards of his community. Just as an anthropologist finds the mores of primitive tribes to be inexplicable or irrational, so a social isolate in modern communities will query ideas and values that the main body of society accepts without question.

People who do not conform may be mocked for their eccentricities, but history is full of examples of the considerable value rendered to the community by people who have questioned old and unbroken traditions. An eccentric suggests that there may be another way of looking at things – outside the central view – and thus becomes a non-conformist, and then an innovator.

Fundamental changes affecting the whole social pattern now occur within the life of a single individual and innovators are required to produce new ideas to fit new situations. This is happening just as often in the field of social behaviour as in politics or economics. There has always been a conflict between the non-conformist and the established customs of the community and the progress of society has always depended on this conflict. But the value of people who feel the need to question old moral laws and customs is far greater today than ever before because the pressures towards conformism are stronger and social situations change more rapidly. The rebel against an over-organized authority is often the distinguishing characteristic of the young user of cannabis.

Although non-conformism in individuals is a useful asset to any community, a collection of non-conformists driven into social isolation, forming an introverted minority group, is not a constructive entity. It is a union against the dominant majority and so it is more likely to be an irritant than an aid to the well-being of the community.

Social Pressures

The standard of behaviour in some of the cannabis-orientated groups is high. But the new member of even the most circumspect cannabis coterie must discard many of the social controls which are part of the outside world in favour of the less conventional attitudes of the in-group. Before long all the ties which are important to him are with other cannabis users. The group has its own status symbols and mythology, and provides the same kind of psychological support that a family group provides for other people. This means that he becomes alienated from the conventional culture. It gradually becomes more and more difficult for him to be a participant in community activities even in a limited way. From a social isolate he becomes a social alien.

All this is exacerbated by the generation gap that separates the cannabis coteries from the community. Religious, racial, even homosexual groups do not have this age division. The youth versus age factor is a particular characteristic of the drug problem. One of the more famous sayings in the cannabis coteries is 'don't trust anyone over thirty'. This means that the ideas within these introverted groups are likely to be inexperienced and immature. It also prompts the question: what happens to the pot smoker after he reaches thirty?

It is important to note that the tendency to form these introverted groups is not caused by taking cannabis: it is the result of social hostility. It is almost as if people have an unconscious desire to wall off drug takers from the rest of us. All the pressures of society tend to push the individual users of cannabis into groups of like-minded pot smokers who think of themselves as a persecuted superior minority. This is an ironic situation, because those who are outraged by any suggestion that the cannabis laws should be changed are the very people who are making sure that the cannabis culture will become a strong influence in the life of the community.

Unfortunately this chapter may have given the impression that nearly all users of cannabis will end up in an introverted minority group. It is necessary therefore, to emphasize that this progression hardly applies at all to the sporadic user (Zinberg, 1970). Furthermore there is a large number of regular users who live unharrassed lives and are well integrated with the community. Using a large sample representative of the adult population of San Francisco, Manheimer (1969) found the majority of cannabis users were 'reasonably conventional'. Pot smokers comprise a heterogenous group of personality types, some of whom are respectable and valuable members of the community – at least one is an ex-member of the Cabinet. These people have successfully achieved this balance between the normal world and the cannabis culture *despite* the social pressures and the tendency to regard all drug takers as outcasts. Psychiatrists and others who meet a pot smoker search for a flaw in the personality, but the severest problems are created by imperfections in society, not in the individual.

It is now a well-established sociological principle (Westwood, 1960; Becker, 1963; Matza, 1969) that people regarded as deviants will become deviant, not because of their type of behaviour, but as a result of the social hostility to their preferred activities. The extent to which an individual can resist these social pressures depends upon his personality and on the defences he erects against this social hostility. The effect of these pressures is a matter of degree, but the direction is always the same – away from integration with the community.

13

Law Enforcement

Public Pressures

The social hostility described in the last chapter is, of course, not vindictive, but a genuine fear that drugs are a danger to the well-being of the community. There is some foundation for this, but intermixed with these fears is the ignorant idea that one drug is much like another, and misinformation about the extent and effects of drug use.

This public disquiet influences the police and the judiciary who are expected to reflect the changing views of the community. The public and the press demand that the law enforcement authorities 'do something' about the so-called drug problem, which, in fact, comprises many different problems. This places great pressure on the police to take action, which in turn affects the conduct of individual policemen and encourages over-zealous actions which, in some instances, may be unjust or even illegal. At the same time the severity of penalties for cannabis offences and the widespread belief in the escalation theory cause misunderstanding in the minds of the judiciary.

Although the number of drug offences is minute compared to the total number of all offences, the proportion of cannabis offences to other drugs is significant. There were 6,095 convictions under the (1965) Dangerous Drugs Act in 1969; of these, 4,683 (77 per cent) were cannabis offences. In the same year there were 7,101 convictions for possessing all types of illegal drugs, of which 4,094 (57 per cent) were for possessing cannabis. So more people are convicted for taking cannabis than for any other drug.

In 1967 a more detailed analysis was made of the cannabis

offences. It was found that over two thirds of all cannabis offenders
did not have a record of non-drug offences. Nine out of ten of all
cannabis offences were for possessing less than 30 grams. About a
quarter of all cannabis offenders were sent to prison and 17 per
cent of first offenders were imprisoned. Even those convicted of
possessing small amounts of cannabis run the risk of being dealt
with quite severely. The figures given in the fourth section of
chapter 4 revealed that three in every twenty persons convicted of
possessing less than 30 grams of cannabis were imprisoned.

These are very striking figures. They make it clear that young
people without criminal records are being severely punished for
possessing very small amounts of cannabis. It makes nonsense of
the occasional police statement that they are only interested in
catching the dealers. It shows that magistrates have failed to
appreciate the difference between cannabis and other drugs. This
analysis was made three years ago and there are signs that there
has been some improvement since then, but the reception given to
the Wootton report does not suggest that chief constables or
magistrates will find it easy to alter their previous attitudes to
cannabis.

Police Discretion

Most people do not realize that the police have very wide powers of
discretion. Indeed they have to be given this discretion because it
is impossible to enforce all the laws all the time and so small
police forces with limited budgets have to select and choose sensibly. The result is that chief constables have become extremely
powerful. There are now so many laws that if only a fraction of
them were fully enforced, the courts of this country would be
absolutely overwhelmed. In many instances it is neither Parliament, nor the Government, but rather an individual chief constable who decides what the law of the land should be in his
borough.

The 1963 Gaming Act is an example of a law that the police
decided not to enforce. In 1968 the Minister of Transport was
bluntly told by the chief constables' traffic committee that roadside

noise meters were 'unworkable' and they did not intend to use them. Variations in the attitudes of local chief constables make for very big differences in the way the law is administered. In York 756 motorists were cautioned for speeding in 1967, 2,588 in 1966. In Middlesbrough, a town half as big again, one was cautioned in 1967, two in 1966. In Torbay a new police superintendent has decided that there will be no more 'public dancing in clubs and hotels on Sundays'. In other places like Bournemouth and Brighton it is allowed because the police exercise their discretion in a different way. In Manchester there was one prosecution for importuning in 1955, none in 1956 and 1957, two in 1958. A new chief constable was appointed at the end of that year and the number of prosecutions rose to 30 in 1959, to 105 in 1960, to 135 in 1961 and to 216 in 1962.

Although each chief constable has his own bias and prejudices like everyone else, the system works quite well because these powers of discretion usually reflect the changing attitudes of the public. But it is important to realize how great these powers are, and to recognize the influences that may lead to an abuse of these powers.

The alarm about drugs began a few years ago at about the same time as the good relations between public and police started to decline. Furthermore the reputation of the police was waning as the number of crimes soared and the conviction rate slumped. The public demanded that the authorities get tough with the drug takers and the police saw this as an excellent opportunity to regain some of their lost prestige. They also thought that it would be relatively easy to catch a real drug addict because he has to have regular supplies from an illegal source, and he would get careless and inefficient as he becomes more dependent on the drug. It was decided, therefore, to devote large expenditures of police time and money on a campaign against drug offenders and this was expected to produce a quick and easy boost to the conviction rates – one of the yardsticks by which the performance of chief constables is judged.

The individual policeman soon becomes aware of the particular interest of his chief and probably shares the public alarm about drugs. He believes, as many do, that the right way to deal with the problem is to stamp it out with all the powers at his command and therefore he is open to the temptation to bend the rules to secure the conviction of an individual whom he honestly suspects of having committed a drug offence.

The result is that there have been many examples of what the police euphemistically refer to as 'stretching a point'. This has led to a large number of allegations of police malpractices. Drug offences are consensual crimes and there is rarely a victim or an aggrieved party. Consequently it is more difficult for the police to obtain evidence, so sometimes they have to resort to using informers or decoys. Persons arrested for drug offences are sometimes pressurized into helping to trap other users. They are persuaded to ring up a friend to arrange a bogus sale, or to supply cannabis to a suspect who is then promptly arrested for possession. If they do not agree to aid the police in this way, they may be told that bail will be opposed or that extra charges will be brought against them.

On other occasions the evidence may be improperly obtained, perhaps by force, duress, false promises or failure to caution the defendant before he makes a statement. The police may also bargain with the accused and urge him to plead guilty in return for a quick trial or a light sentence – suggestions which might influence a first offender, although an experienced criminal would know that the police do not have the power to make these arrangements.

Planting

The most serious allegation is that policemen plant drugs while carrying out a search. It is extremely difficult to find out the truth behind these allegations. Defending lawyers are usually reluctant to allege planting by the police. Some magistrates assume that an accusation against the police is the last resort of a criminal who cannot think of any other excuse.

Coon and Harris (1969), who probably have more experience of this subject than anyone else, report that the number of drug offenders who claim to have been planted is smaller than they expected, but there were a few cases where all the circumstances indicated that the police had used this method to obtain a conviction against a suspect. They felt that persons with a record of previous drug offences were particularly liable to the risk of planting.

One example, cited by the National Council for Civil Liberties, concerned public premises which were being used by a group of young people for rehearsals. The group had been subjected to frequent but unsuccessful searches on previous occasions. The premises had been thoroughly cleaned by the owner, to whom no suspicion of drugs possession could be attached, only a short time before the arrival of the police. Quantities of cannabis were found in other parts of the premises and the group was charged. They elected to go for trial by jury and the magistrate upheld a submission by the defence lawyers that there was no case to answer on the grounds that there was no proof that the drugs belonged to them. So the issue of how the drugs got there did not arise as the case did not go to trial.

A very well-known pop star told me that when his house was raided by the police, they searched the whole house, at first without success. But after a second visit to a room upstairs, a policeman claimed to have found a wrapped brick of hash. The house owner had never seen it before. Later still his own small supply of cannabis was produced and subsequently the first find was never mentioned when he was charged, nor when the case came to court. His theory is that the press were already aware of the raid and it would have been embarrassing for the police if they had not managed to find an illegal drug on the premises; but after getting what they were looking for, they decided not to say anything about the drug they had planted.

Of course it is impossible to substantiate any of these allegations. Even in the rare cases when a verdict of not guilty has been returned after police planting has been put forward as the defence, it is still not possible to assume that this is proof that the police were to blame. It is quite difficult for the court to censure the police even if it is believed that the police had planted the drug. When the trial is before a jury the court cannot say anything before the verdict is given because it is not known whether the defence is valid or not; after the verdict is given the court does not know why the defendant was found not guilty, and there is no further opportunity to comment. The court cannot comment on the action of the police unless that is the issue to be tried.

My own view is that as it is an easy allegation to make, all accusations of planting should be treated with caution, and probably most should be discounted. But there are a few cases where the evidence does lead one to suspect planting and this should be the cause of considerable disquiet. Accusations of planting are rarely believed and very difficult to prove. This is all the more reason why we should take these allegations very seriously, because the individual policeman must know that if he does plant a drug on an innocent person his offence is not likely to be detected. His own conscience and his sense of justice are the only deterrents.

I have met honest policemen who will admit that planting does occur on rare occasions, saying that even in the police force there are bound to be some bad characters. But this is not a satisfactory explanation. If you are content to allow a few innocent people to be planted in the interests of catching drug addicts and traffickers, then you should be reminded that the next innocent person to be planted may be you.

Police Malpractices

The Dangerous Drugs Act, 1967, section 6 (1), gave the police powers to search anyone they have 'reasonable grounds' for suspecting of carrying drugs. The police seem to have interpreted this law to mean that they have a right to make random searches. Long hair, unconventional dress, youthful appearance, and being out on the streets after midnight are all considered by the police to be reasonable grounds. Any young person can be stopped and searched for no other reason than that they are perceived as part of a suspect generation. Their pockets will be gone through and, if the police are not convinced of their innocence, they will be taken to the police station for a more thorough search. There have been large-scale raids on teenage clubs in which everyone on the premises has been searched.

Police raids on clubs where there are a hundred or more present seem to be particularly ineffective. It is quite easy for those who do have drugs in their possession to get rid of them. Most people would throw them on the floor, but there is also the danger that they might slip them into someone else's pocket while waiting to be searched in an unsupervised group, with the result that the wrong person is charged with being in possession.

The Deedes committee was set up to inquire into these allegations of excessive zeal by the police, but the phrase 'reasonable grounds' cannot be adequately defined and only a limitation on the power to stop and search without a warrant would provide the necessary safeguards to our civil liberties. The only 'reasonable' ground for searching a person is specific information which leads the policeman to suspect that drugs are being used or carried.

If a substance is found which the officer suspects is an illegal drug, it is sent away to a police forensic laboratory to be analysed. This may take up to three weeks. In some cases the person is arrested and charged even before the substance has been identified by an analyst. If for some reason he is not granted bail, he may be kept in custody until his case is heard. If it turns out to be a legal substance, he will be brought before the court and freed. A better system is to put the defendant on 'police' bail. This means he is required to report to the police station on a particular day. If the analysis shows the substance is illegal, he will be charged with the appropriate offence when he returns to the station. If he fails to appear, a warrant can be issued for his arrest. If the substance is not illegal, no time will have been spent unnecessarily in court.

Sometimes charges are based on trace elements on such articles as pipes and ashtrays. Such very small amounts of cannabis are unconvincing evidence of possession because it is impossible to assess precisely when the drug was used.

There have been many complaints that when a person is taken to the police station on a drugs charge, he is refused the right to make a telephone call to his family, a friend or solicitor. In other cases it has been suggested that the police make the call for the defendant and tell him that the line was engaged or there was no answer; later checks have shown that the persons called were available at the time the police said they telephoned. In the Release report (1969) it is concluded that 'this obstruction is deliberate, in order to prevent arrangements being made for bail and defence. A young person in custody who has been denied access to a telephone is much more easily subdued and induced to plead guilty.'

The right to make at least one call should be universally observed at police stations and persistent attempts should be made to get through even if a line is temporarily engaged or a call is not answered immediately. It must be assumed that the probability is that an arrested person would want to contact a solicitor or a friend. If for some reason this is not the case, the accused should sign a statement to say that he does not want to contact anyone outside the police station.

There appear to be no restrictions on the materials and objects which the police may seize during the search of private premises. Such items as address books are often retained on the grounds that they are needed as exhibits. People have been contacted and searched where there have been no grounds for suspicion other than that their names and addresses have been found in the home of a person arrested on a drugs charge.

The police evidence on the amount of cannabis seized is often misleading. They place a monetary value on the amount seized and this is often exaggerated because it is based on the market value of the smallest unit. Last February the press reported that three sacks of cannabis resin were found in the funnel of a ship at Tilbury docks. All the newspapers gave the value of the cannabis as £300,000 and this was the figure given later in court. In fact the three sacks contained 336 pounds of resin which would fetch between £15,000 and £20,000 if sold as one lot; if broken down into one ounce packages it might sell at £9 an ounce, making a maximum value of £50,000. The police should state the amount seized in grams so as to leave no room for misunderstanding.

Sometimes the police claim to have found less cannabis than they have seized and taken away. If they state in court that the accused had 15 grams when in fact they found 25 grams, the defendant is not likely to get up and say he had more. Perhaps the police need a supply of cannabis in order to train their dogs, but this method of obtaining an unauthorized supply does increase the possibilities of planting. Seized drugs are supposed to be destroyed under the supervision of a senior police officer and special care should be taken to make sure that all that is seized is destroyed.

Police Attitude to Allegations

The usual police reply to these allegations is that they are not substantiated. This is true. It is almost impossible to prove allegations of police malpractices and this is exactly why special safeguards are required to protect the rights of the citizen.

Whenever allegations are made against the police, they are denied. There exists a powerful fellowship in the force which persuades a policeman to stick up for all other policemen; this has many advantages, but it often looks to the outsider like bland overconfidence in the unshakeable belief that nothing ever goes wrong in the police force.

The official remedy for dealing with abuses of police authority is the complaint procedure under section 49 of the 1964 Act. If someone charges the police with misbehaviour, he is usually asked at the station if his complaint is formal or informal. If it is the latter, no more will be heard about it and he must assume appropriate disciplinary measures have been taken. If it is to be an official complaint, the matter is investigated by a senior police officer. This means that the police act as both judge and jury when they themselves are accused. Where criminal offences are alleged, the case will be referred to the Director of Public Prosecutions, but he is unlikely to act unless the evidence against the police officers is substantial. When other policemen are the only witnesses, the likelihood of obtaining such evidence is remote.

A defendant is usually advised not to make complaints about the police because this may prejudice his case in the eyes of a magistrate. If the result of the case is a finding of guilty, although the accused may still maintain his innocence and may still complain of police malpractices, normally most people regard it as rather futile to lodge an official complaint after an unfavourable verdict from a magistrate or jury. Having exhausted any appeal structure through the courts, they feel they are not likely to achieve anything by trying to raise the same issue in another forum.

If found not guilty the defendant may wish to forget about the matter as quickly as possible or may be deterred from taking further action by the difficulties of taking civil or criminal proceedings against the officers concerned. An independent complaints procedure would remove some of the difficulties and create more confidence that complaints are dealt with adequately.

When an accusation is made against the police, the individual case must be investigated. But more important than this, senior officers should ask, not only did it happen, but could it happen. If there is the possibility of police malpractice, senior officers should cooperate with others in an attempt to devise a system of safeguards so that it cannot happen and the police cannot be subjected to these accusations. Of course it is not always possible to devise such safeguards, and then we are forced to strike a balance between the efficiency of the police and the rights of the citizen.

The drug user is also a citizen. As the law stands he is a criminal, but he still has certain rights. It is not a question of police corruption, brutality or other gross miscarriage of justice. It is a quieter, more insidious kind of injustice; bending the law a little bit in one case, forgetting a regulation in a second, being too busy to attend to someone's legitimate request in a third.

The police must know, but seem to have forgotten, that they simply cannot carry out their tasks without public cooperation and before long they are going to need the goodwill of these citizens of tomorrow. Young people between fifteen and twenty-five are very impressionable and the growing alienation between this on-coming generation and the police is ominous.

Judges and Magistrates

It is important that laws enacted by Parliament be enforced, but it is of equal importance that the safeguards woven into such laws be respected. When these safeguards are ignored in a significant number of cases, it is up to the judiciary to ensure strict compliance with the restrictions on police powers and the rights of the citizen.

In practice it is quite difficult for the judiciary to carry out this function. For example, if telephone contact is refused or obstructed while the accused is in the police station and this matter is reported to the magistrate, he could draw it to the attention of the chief officer concerned. In fact the court rarely comments on the action of the police unless this is the matter being tried. It is perfectly possible for a person to be found guilty, and be guilty, even though the police behaviour was incorrect. When a person is found not guilty, the court is unlikely to say that this is because the police acted improperly.

When the allegations are disputed, the magistrates usually believe the police. This is understandable. They work with the police every day; in the normal course of events the arresting officer is more likely to tell the truth than the defendant; criticism from a magistrate lowers morale in the police force which is already overworked and undermanned. Nevertheless it should not be forgotten that the policeman is well aware that his evidence will nearly always be believed and this must tempt some officers to exaggerate and fabricate.

It is to be expected that the police are anxious to make the charge stick once they have taken a man in. But magistrates should make sure that this attitude is not taken too far, especially when it is used to defend rough justice such as – 'Well, maybe he didn't have a drug on him this time, but we know he smokes pot.'

Magistrates need to show more care before issuing search warrants. The Home Secretary has recently issued a warning to chief officers of police of the dangers of applying for search warrants on the basis of anonymous information. David Napley of the Law Society wrote in a letter to *The Times*:[1]

For the most part warrants – both for arrest and search – appear, throughout the country, to be issued in a perfunctory fashion. So long as an officer swears to the truth of the written and sparse information on which his application for a warrant is based, it often appears to be granted without inquiry and as a matter of course. Too many magistrates, although by no means all, pay insufficient regard to the fact that Parliament both intended and decreed that they – and not the police –

1. 4 March 1968.

need to be satisfied that reasonable grounds of suspicion exist to justify interference with the liberty or privacy of the public.

Magistrates need to inquire more closely into the evidence on which applications are based.

The police should report back to the magistrate who granted the warrant after its execution. It is possible that magistrates may not be in a very good position to assess the information put before them and if they are always given a report on the results of the search, they will acquire more knowledge and expertise. For example, the reports might show that a particular individual had been providing inaccurate information over a period and this would make a magistrate more suspicious when granting a warrant on information from this source in the future. An additional advantage in establishing efficient recording and reporting-back procedures is that the resulting statistics would provide a broad national picture of the situation, which is not available at present.

It is not unknown for police officers to arrive at premises without a warrant and wrongly to effect and sometimes virtually to force an entry, particularly when the drug suspect is young and unaware of his rights. If defending lawyers bring this to the notice of the courts, it should be the subject of severe criticism; for it is possible that the police will be tempted to plant drugs if they do not find any, so as to justify their illegal entry.

Bail

As all cases involving drugs have to wait until the substance has been analysed and this may take as long as three weeks, the question of bail assumes greater importance than in many other cases. The problem is exacerbated because the police are empowered to grant bail to persons charged with the possession of drugs.

Sometimes the defendants are urged to plead guilty in return for bail being granted. The accused is told that if he makes a statement admitting his guilt, then he will be released that evening; but if he is not going to be helpful, then he will have to be brought before the magistrates in the morning and he will have to spend the night in custody. In effect the police are saying, if you are guilty you can go, but if you are innocent you must stay overnight in the police cell. It is quite illogical but this is what happens.

If the defendant refuses this offer, the application to the magistrate for bail may be opposed by the police. In theory substantial reasons must be given by the police when they object to bail, but all available statistics show that their advice is taken in the vast majority of cases. A magistrate may be satisfied by the vague statement 'we have not completed our inquiries' and comply with police objections to bail.

Even if the magistrate overrules the police and does grant bail, the prisoner cannot be released until he has a suitable surety. The police can object to anyone who presents himself in this capacity. Without the cooperation of the police it is difficult for a person to get bail, even after the magistrate has granted it, because the only contact with the outside world for someone in custody is through the police.

Sometimes friends and relatives refuse to stand surety because they are under the mistaken impression that money has to be produced immediately: 'The mother of a seventeen-year-old girl who had been granted bail but sent to Holloway to await the arrival of her surety, was asked if she could stand £50 bail for her daughter. She refused thinking she had to be able to find the £50 in cash which she did not have' (Coon and Harris, 1969).

Persons arrested for possessing drugs are often young, living with friends away from their parents in furnished accommodation where they may have been for only a short time, and may be regarded by the police as being of no fixed abode. Others mislead the police into believing they have no fixed address in order to protect their friends and do not realize this decreases their chances of getting bail.

Once a person has appeared in court and has been remanded in custody, it is extremely difficult for the accused to arrange bail. It is possible to write a letter from the remand centre or prison, but many young people do not understand the procedure and do not know the address of anyone who can help. The police can undertake to contact sureties but their attempts can hardly be described as enthusiastic.

The result is that a considerable number of persons arrested for drug offences spend a period, possibly of weeks, in custody, irrespective of whether they are subsequently acquitted or convicted and not sent to prison. If the defendant elects to go for trial by jury or is taken before a higher court because of the seriousness of his case, his remand in custody is likely to be a matter of months. Even a short time in custody can lead to considerable disruption including loss of employment, and may be the direct cause of a person forsaking normal society in favour of a drug-orientated group.

Bail should not be opposed by the police, and should be granted in all but the most exceptional cases. If bail is granted and sureties are not arranged within two or three hours, the magistrate concerned should be informed. The only reasonable objection to bail is that the accused is likely to abscond. In situations where an individual is arrested for possession of small amounts of cannabis, he should be allowed bail on his own recognizance. When it is absolutely necessary to keep a person in custody, a special priority should be arranged so that the substance is analysed immediately and the case brought before the court without further delay.

The Deedes Report

A few members of the Deedes sub-committee were worried about the situation brought to light by the evidence summarized quite fairly in the first 96 paragraphs of the report. But the majority felt that the drugs problem was so serious that the police should be given maximum powers and should not be restricted in any way. Although there might be isolated examples of malpractices in the police and injustice in the courts, the majority believed that the situation was generally so satisfactory that things could be left as they were.

Consequently the recommendations of the majority were largely negative. The only positive proposals were:

1. Better records should be kept on police searches carried out with or without a warrant.
2. The police must accept that modes of dress or hair style do

not by themselves constitute reasonable grounds to stop and search a suspected drugs offender.

3. It is better to defer making a charge until the seized substance has been analysed. When a suspected drugs offender is held in custody, the analysis should be made available within forty-eight hours.

4. The Home Office should think about providing a suspect with a leaflet explaining his legal rights.

The minority were in favour of repealing the police powers to stop and search altogether. They felt that the police should be instructed to grant bail to all cannabis offenders solely on their own recognizance. They believed that all persons accused of possessing illegal drugs should have the right to contact a solicitor or friend. They also wished to impose some restrictions on the authority of the police to seize documents belonging to suspected drug offenders.

Inevitably it was a very divided report which contained views which were irreconcilable. It may have some effect on the final shape of the new drugs legislation and it is a valuable document because it has brought several problems to the notice of the general public. But there are still many cases where the rights of suspected drugs offenders are in jeopardy.

Justice and Drugs Offenders

When a young person is arrested for a drugs offence, it is unlikely that he will get a fair hearing unless he is represented by a lawyer. Everyone is entitled to apply for legal aid but the magistrate's power to grant it is quite arbitrary; if a plea of guilty is anticipated, it is more likely to be refused (Paterson, 1970). But even in those cases it is better to have someone to speak on behalf of the defendant who pleads guilty; a lawyer can make a plea of mitigation or put an end to obstructive police behaviour.

The police often tell the accused that he does not need a solicitor. Undefended cases mean less work for the police; their evidence is uncontested and a conviction is more likely. The presence of a defending lawyer forces the police to be more accurate and more discriminating in the charges they press. Lawyers can make arrangements with the police and are often successful in getting charges dropped before cases come to court.

Sometimes the defendant does not know a solicitor and then the clerk of the court chooses one for him if he is granted legal aid. This is not always a good arrangement. The chosen solicitor may be well known by the court and the police, and this may not be in the best interests of the defendant.

The Release report notes the importance of being middle class if you are going to be arrested for a drugs offence. Young people from working-class backgrounds are at a definite disadvantage; they are less articulate, less likely to be legally represented, less prepared to ignore the advice of the police, and are more likely to get a prison sentence. People of higher education can speak for themselves, can gain access to a lawyer, and are more likely to get probation or a conditional discharge.

If the possession of cannabis is a crime which is thought to be serious enough to bear the penalty of a prison sentence on a first offence, a solicitor should be automatically available to a defendant. People ought not to be sent to prison without being legally advised.

Judges and magistrates share the same attitudes to drugs as the general public. This is not a cause for concern, but it does mean that a certain amount of ignorance and prejudice will be found. Youth has always been in revolt and their social defiance is often expressed as particular styles of dress, language, music, political protest, minor forms of delinquency or a relaxed attitude to sexual behaviour. All these forms of youthful rebellion have disturbed and sometimes annoyed adults in one way or another, though most have managed to tolerate them even if they did not understand them. But drug taking is an altogether different matter which older people have found far more deeply bewildering and disturbing. This is partly explained by the newness and puzzling nature of the phenomenon. The ironic result is that in a court of law the accused is usually better informed about drugs than the magistrate.

This means that the magistracy and the judiciary must take extra care in order to preserve the defendant's safeguards and ensure justice. Even if it can be shown during the court hearing that malpractices have occurred before the person was charged with the drugs offence, the court usually takes the view that, whatever the irregularities, the case now being before the court, the trial should proceed, leaving the accused to pursue such civil remedies as may be available to him. If the defendant is convicted, these civil remedies are in fact illusory, as it would be almost impossible to bring a successful civil action no matter how serious the malpractices may have been. In the United States evidence improperly obtained would be excluded, but here the law tends to regard the end as justifying the means.

This is in sharp contrast to the decisions of judges and magistrates when dealing with the breathalyzer and the Road Safety Act 1967. Until a very recent decision in the courts, it had become clear that if the safeguards were not strictly observed, the arrest was illegal and a conviction could not be sustained. Thus it appears to young people that police behaviour must be absolutely circumspect when dealing with alcohol, the drug of the older generation, but the law can be bent when dealing with cannabis, the drug of the younger generation.

The Legal Objectives

Most people believe that the use of cannabis is contrary to the best interests of society, and the law is intended to prohibit its use. This objective may still be valid although it has been shown that the most usual arguments against cannabis are based on misconceptions and misinformation. We now know that the effects of taking cannabis are not harmful in normal circumstances. It is also clear that its use does not lead to addictive hard drugs, crime or sexual orgies.

But there are still good reasons for retaining the law against cannabis, even though it may not be necessary to attach such serious sanctions to its use and possession. The main arguments against legalization are:

(1) The use of all new recreational drugs should be discouraged. Even if cannabis is more benign in its effects than alcohol, it would still be a mistake to add another non-therapeutic drug to those already and irreversibly legalized.

(2) Britain is a party to the 1961 Single Convention on Narcotic Drugs and it would be wrong to abandon the prohibition of cannabis after signing this international agreement.

(3) Even though it may have been inappropriate to control cannabis under the Dangerous Drugs Acts, a big reduction in the penalties would appear to condone the smoking of cannabis.

(4) No matter what the experts may say about cannabis, public opinion is not yet ready for any liberalization in the law.

These are strong arguments. But there is some doubt if the law is realizing its objectives or contributing towards a solution to the problem of cannabis. There are nine important reasons for looking at the law again to see if it can be improved. (1) The concept of possession is clumsy. (2) The law misinforms. (3) It is expensive. (4) It is capricious. (5) It gives rise to a sense of injustice. (6) It is ineffective. (7) It is the cause of social alienation. (8) It widens the generation gap. (9) There are better ways of achieving the same objectives. These nine criticisms of the law will be considered briefly in this chapter.

The Concept of Possession

It is claimed that a law which is concerned with possession is the best way to catch the sellers of drugs, but such a law leads inevitably to accusations of planting, whether they be true or false. In fact most people are arrested, not because they are found smoking cannabis, but because it is found in their possession. Of the 4,683 convicted of cannabis offences in 1969, 4,094 (87 per cent) were for the offence of possession; only 147 (3 per cent) were found guilty of supplying cannabis.

The concept of possession is particularly cumbersome when someone is said to be in possession of something when it is not actually found on him and where the actual location of the drug is equivocal as far as the person is concerned. It may be found in the room where he is at the time although this may not be his home; it may be found in a car which he is alleged to have driven shortly before the drug was discovered. Although there is evidence given in court of the drug being found in a certain place, that evidence taken in isolation would not be conclusive and it often depends on the remarks which the police claim the accused made at the time. This is often disputed in court and very often the decision of the court depends upon the question of what was said or not said by the accused.

If it is possible to keep some control over alcohol without making it illegal for people to carry it about, at least an attempt might be made to frame a law without making the *possession* of drugs an offence. It might be possible to make the law similar to the 'drunk and disorderly' enactments, particularly for the less harmful drugs. Ideally the criterion should be the behaviour of the man whilst under the influence of a drug, not whether he has some grains of a specific drug in his possession. If he is aggressive or a nuisance, then the law should step in to restrain him. But if he is not causing trouble to anyone or to society in general, then it is hard to see why the law should interfere.

The Law Misinforms

There may be controversy over the effects of cannabis, but nearly everyone would agree that it is less harmful than the other major illegal drugs. This was emphasized by the Wootton committee who reported that the legal association of cannabis with heroin and other opiates was 'entirely inappropriate' and that the effects of the use of cannabis were 'intrinsically different' from those of other drugs.

We now know that both the international treaty and the British law which followed it was based on misinformation. It might be said that this does not matter so long as the end result is satisfactory. But this situation presents the education authorities with an impossible task.

Many commentators conclude that the best solution to the drug problem is more and better education. Indeed it is offered as a solution to most of our more intractable problems. But what is the teacher supposed to say about cannabis? If he says that it is not a very harmful drug, he will be accused of condoning cannabis. If he followed the textbooks and produces a list of the horrible results that can follow from the use of cannabis, he will not be believed. As cannabis is the most controversial of all the restricted drugs, he cannot evade the question.

Even the proposed legislation fails to make an adequate distinction between cannabis and the other recreational drugs. This is undesirable for social and medical reasons, and places an additional strain on those who enforce the law.

The Cost of this Law

Over two thirds of cannabis offenders are otherwise law-abiding citizens. Thus we are 'criminalizing' over 2,000 people each year and this involves a very high social cost. There is the material cost of enforcing the law and the psychological cost of turning a large number of young people into criminals.

All laws are expensive to administer, but the cost is usually thought to be outweighed by the benefits. But there must be some doubt whether the cost of detecting and arresting over 3,000 cannabis offenders is really worth while. The work of the courts is already overtaxed, but all of these cases must come before the court at least twice, and some of them three, four or more times.

The increase in cannabis offences is very recent; ten years ago there were less than 250. The average policeman knows very little about this new crime and in several areas chief constables have found it necessary to form special drug squads with policemen working full time on the problem. There are probably more people chasing, arresting and treating drug takers than there are heroin addicts in this country. Some people wonder whether this expenditure on judicial and police resources could be better applied elsewhere.

There are other social costs which are less easy to measure. If a man is arrested for possessing cannabis, he will probably lose his job and he will find it difficult to get another one. This experience will decrease his respect for the law, especially if he feels that his crime has not hurt anyone. If he is sent to prison or borstal, he will come into contact with experienced criminals and upon release he may find it easier to associate with these people than go back to his old friends, some of whom will ostracize him.

The existence of these high costs does not mean, in itself, that it is a bad law. But it is a factor to be taken into consideration when judging the efficiency of a law, especially as this public expenditure is likely to increase each year as more and more people use cannabis. Therefore it is necessary to ask if these social and psychological costs are a worth-while investment.

The Law is Capricious

There is also a wide variation in the sentences awarded for similar cannabis offences. Working-class boys appear to get more severe penalties. Defending lawyers still have to warn their clients that the sentence they get may depend upon their clothes or the length of their hair.

For every pot smoker known to the police there are hundreds that are undetected. Whether a cannabis user becomes involved with the law depends in part only upon his actions; it may also depend upon some influential segment of the community that becomes concerned about a particular state of affairs and brings pressure to bear on the police to take action. It will also depend upon the attitude of the chief constable in the particular area in which the pot smoker lives; some act as if they accept the findings in the Wootton report, others exhibit a crusading zeal to stamp out all signs of cannabis.

This gives the police wide discretion and allows them to arrest some people for cannabis offences because they feel they should be dealt with for entirely different reasons. This law can be used to curb political dissent or to suppress someone whose defiance of authority is embarrassing but not illegal. The police drive against several well-known pop singers had the appearance of a vendetta against a particular life style which was thought to be a bad example to the young.

There has been more than one case in which a person's home has been searched and nothing found; when a complaint about police behaviour was received, the place was promptly raided again and this time an illegal drug was found. In several areas the coloured residents are convinced that the police are more likely to stop and search them than the white people who live in the district.

The Law Creates a Genuine Sense of Injustice

It is always necessary to strike a balance between the civil liberties of the subject and the necessity to enforce the law. The more serious the crime, the more freedom should be given to the police. But when it is a victimless crime and when the opportunities of police malpractice are considerable, then the rights of the citizen are paramount and safeguards are needed.

The law on drugs, and on cannabis in particular, is a constant source for allegations of planting, entrapment, and the use of informers or decoys; there is also the suspicion that not all confiscated drugs are destroyed. No doubt the dangers of corruption in this area are fully realized by police authorities and precautions taken, but there are still more allegations of bribery than one would expect for a crime which does not increase the offender's wealth. The fact that abuses are hard to prove means that they are more likely to flourish.

Two famous cases in recent years serve as examples. In the summer of 1967 Mick Jagger was charged with possessing four tablets containing drugs which he had bought quite legally in Italy but which were illegal in Britain without prescription. He had been granted bail at committal proceedings, but was kept in custody at the end of the first day's trial. On the second morning of the trial, while still unconvicted, he was brought from prison in handcuffs. It was agreed during the course of the trial that the police had at all times received full cooperation from Jagger. Although the charges against the two other defendants were quite different, none of the three accused were sentenced until the evidence against all three had been completed. On the third day Jagger was kept in the cells all day awaiting sentence. There was no justification for any of these procedures and it appears that the object was to vilify this famous pop star in the eyes of the younger generation. The 'exemplary' sentence given for this unimportant conviction on a technicality caused an outcry in the press and on appeal Jagger was given a conditional discharge. Two years later Jagger was arrested for possessing cannabis. On this occasion he alleged that the drug was planted and a policeman suggested bribery. He was convicted and fined, and the police rejected his allegations.

The second case concerns Lady Diana Cooper whose flat was raided in 1968. The police had a search warrant and no complaint was made about their behaviour inside the house. But because this was the house of a well-known personality, there was a special debate in the House of Commons (7 March 1968) about this incident which was, in fact, similar to hundreds of other raids carried out by the police over the years. Later Lady Diana received a personal visit and an apology from the Deputy Commissioner of the Metropolitan Police, and the Home Secretary circulated a special note to chief officers of police asking them to be more careful before applying for search warrants. The Lord Chancellor issued a similar note to those responsible for the training of magistrates.

Both these cases received wide publicity, but there are many cases of police malpractice which do not get reported in the press. One example of this was a case which came to the notice of the Law Society. The short facts of the case are as follows: It had come to the knowledge of the police that a man who had been convicted and sent to prison for possessing drugs was due to be released from prison on a particular day. Apparently on no greater evidence than this, the police sought and obtained a search warrant for premises to which it was known that he was intending to return. They duly entered the premises, without difficulty, having sought admission at the door. Within the premises were a number of persons of good character, each of whom was a graduate of a university. The police then directed the women present to go to one room and the men to another; required the men to stand against the wall with their hands upon their heads, and the women to be searched by a woman police officer. It was the contention of the occupants of the property that they did not object to the police enforcing a warrant which, on the face of it, appeared to be have been regularly issued, but they greatly resented the tone and manner in which they were accosted and the indignity to which they were subjected, as was alleged, by force. A young woman was found in possession of 1½ dexedrine tablets which she had taken for slimming purposes and with which she was subsequently charged. Another had pills prescribed for epilepsy, which were not made the subject of a charge. No other dangerous drugs were found whatsoever but, arising out of their protests at the manner of search used by the officers, charges were brought under section 14 (3) of the Dangerous

Drugs Act of wilfully obstructing police officers in the exercise of their powers. Despite a strong contest, all the defendants were in due course convicted although only nominal penalties were imposed.

The Law is Ineffective

All the arguments in favour of the law assume that it works, but in fact the drugs legislation, as it applies to cannabis, is singularly ineffective. None of the arrangements for treatment in special centres under the 1967 Act applies to cannabis users, because most doctors do not attempt to treat pot smokers. Less than one in ten of those convicted under the 1965 Act are reconvicted for a subsequent drug offence. This may suggest that most first offenders give up cannabis after a conviction for possession; a more probable explanation is that the convictions only reflect a very small proportion of the total number of cannabis users and detection is mostly a matter of chance.

It is obviously impossible to say what proportion of cannabis users are arrested, but a little speculative arithmetic will make clear that hundreds of joints are smoked every day and the chances of getting caught are remote.

The Wootton committee received estimates of the total number of cannabis users which ranged between 30,000 and 300,000.

If one takes a midway figure, we may assume that there are 165,000 pot smokers in the country – probably an underestimate.

Let us assume that each one of these takes cannabis fifty times in a year; therefore there are at least 8,250,000 occasions when the law is being broken.

Leaving aside the significant fact that the police usually arrest people when in possession of the drug, but not when they are smoking it, we know that about 4,000 people were convicted of cannabis offences.

Therefore the chances of being convicted for a cannabis offence are not far greater than 2,000 to one.

This speculative arithmetic is probably wide of the mark, but it does show that the detection rate must be very low. Now it is possible that it will get better if we decide to devote even more police time and expenditure to the task. When President Nixon was elected, one of his first acts was to strengthen the Federal Bureau of Drug Abuse so that a special campaign could be waged against the smuggling of cannabis across the Mexican border. Initially the price of cannabis increased in New York and other large American cities, but the drive against the smugglers was not very successful. It is a long border and a very large number of people are bringing across relatively small amounts. In addition there were protests from ordinary travellers who were subjected to delays and inconvenience at the border.

Even if the Bureau of Drug Abuse had succeeded in curtailing the activities of the dealers, it is not certain that the results would be entirely beneficial. If there was a scarcity of cannabis, this would increase the risk that organized crime, and in particular the Mafia, would gain control of what is at present a loosely organized system of supply. If cannabis were driven off the market, the multiple-drug users would turn to the synthetic drugs which are easier to produce, are less bulky, and can be manufactured within the United States. The amphetamines and barbiturates are quasi-legal and it would be much harder for the Government to build up pressure against these pills because millions of Americans take them on prescription. It is possible that the same situation could occur in this country. If the law against cannabis became more effective, the result might be to increase the consumption of more addictive and dangerous drugs.

In fact the opposite is more likely to happen and the current trend indicates the use of cannabis will continue to spread even though the law is being strictly enforced. Meanwhile the present users of cannabis are growing older, marrying and having children, and are being appointed to important positions in the community. One of the many reasons for the failure of prohibition in the United States was that it became more and more difficult to get jurors to return convictions, because they themselves had often violated the law. Before very long there are going to be pot smokers on the juries who are asked to convict a cannabis offender.

Lenny Bruce once said that cannabis will become legal in a few years time because law students are now smoking it. Eventually there will be lawyers, magistrates and policemen who smoke pot when they are off duty. In the near future there will be parents who take cannabis. Today a teenager can tell his parents he has been invited to a bottle party, but he would not mention an invitation to a pot party. But the parents who smoked cannabis when they were young are likely to be more tolerant and will not be shocked if they find their children using cannabis.

The Law Encourages Social Alienation

The law reflects public attitudes, and at the same time these attitudes are harder to change because of the present state of the law. So the social hostility to cannabis is under-pinned by the law. A tolerant attitude towards users of cannabis is to be 'soft' with criminals; to excuse the smoking of pot is to condone the breaking of the law. Doctors and social workers who are trying to help cannabis smokers who are in some kind of distress have to be ever mindful of their own predicament when trying to assist these law breakers.

The present law does much to ensure that adolescents and young people who take cannabis will be less likely to stop than would otherwise be the case. Because it is illegal they have to get their supplies from someone who, even if he is not a professional pedlar, is likely to be more involved in the drug scene.

If the young pot smoker is arrested, he will be labelled as a drug user and will probably begin to think of himself in this way. All his future behaviour will be influenced by this event. In many cases his family and friends will avoid him and his chances of successful social adjustment will be enormously prejudiced. The effect of appearing in court on a cannabis charge is often calamitous, even if the sentence is not severe. He has to get time off to appear in court and his employer is apt to think there is no smoke without fire. A conditional discharge has led to a man losing his job and future prospects.

The belief in escalation fosters the view that once a person has been arrested for taking cannabis, all hope is lost. Magistrate and judges encourage this view with remarks about cannabis leading on to hard drugs and the young drug offender may come to believe that he will inevitably end up as a heroin addict. If he is imprisoned he will meet, probably for the first time, multiple-drug addicts as well as many other kinds of criminals.

In chapter 13 it was shown that the law tends to push cannabis users into introverted minority groups with strong intra-group loyalties, away from community integration and towards social alienation.

The Law Widens the Generation Gap

One of the most unfortunate things about the controversy over cannabis is that the two sides are so sharply divided by age. Very few people over forty have a good word to say about it, while hundreds of young people think the attitudes of the older generations are hypocritical.

Nearly all cannabis offenders are from the younger sections of the community, whilst of necessity the administration of the law is the responsibility of the older sections. The problem is intensified because the young have received a different and more extensive education, with the result that they are less willing, than heretofore, to agree that laws and policy laid down by the older generations are necessarily wise. They do not believe that the authorities are well informed about cannabis, and the more stringent the laws for its suppression, the more militant they become in defying them.

Furthermore the police find this new spirit among the young makes their job much harder. The police regard the pot-smoking hippy as the epitome of protest and political dissent and so they set about the task of searching and arresting young cannabis users with more than their usual amount of enthusiasm.

In fact the swaggering self-confidence of the young, defiantly asserting their independence, is an outer shell which is tough, but it can collapse at the sight of five policemen and an alsatian dog. Young first offenders are confused and afraid when they run against the law and this is especially true of drug users when they have come down in the cold light of morning. The police station

where the messages never get though; the policemen who obstruct
the search for sureties even after the magistrate has granted bail:
the untrue promises of 'we'll see you get off lightly if you cooperate': these unofficial actions can be countered by the experienced
criminal, but they confuse and depress the young drug offender to
the extent that he does not get the justice he deserves.

Some university staff have noted that the antagonism towards
the police is not confined to the cannabis takers alone. Students
who have no wish to take any drug hear about how their friends
have been treated and resent it. Indeed they may be in danger of
being arrested and charged if they are in the same room as someone
who has a piece of cannabis in his pocket (Hindmarch, 1970).
Young people cannot be expected to ostracize their friends who
occasionally smoke cannabis, even if they do not wish to use it
themselves.

Sometimes the ardent desire of adults to protect the young
merely looks like hypocrisy to them. A girl of sixteen who is
sleeping with a steady partner can be taken 'into care', but the
law does not interfere with an adult woman who is promiscuous.
Similarly, a homosexual of nineteen can be arrested and imprisoned
even if all his sexual activities are with consenting partners in
private. It is as though the young are expected to be better behaved
than adults.

The law on drugs can be used by the police to control the activities and movements of juveniles. Teenage clubs are raided and
young people are taken to the police station to await collection by
their parents. Relations between the police and young people have
never been worse. The cannabis laws are viewed by the young as
just another weapon in the generation war.

The Law does not Provide a Solution

Drug taking is mainly a social problem, less a medical problem.
Legislation can play only a small part in the search for a solution.
It can act as a discovery agency, bringing to the notice of social
workers and doctors those who need help. Otherwise its role is
bound to be very limited.

If a politician thinks that making the law more severe will stamp out the use of cannabis, he is going to be disappointed, but not before many people have been hurt. A man sent to prison for possessing cannabis will not receive any treatment while he is there that will make it any less likely that he will smoke pot on his release. Even a man put on probation will not get any medical treatment; indeed most doctors confess that they do not know what treatment to offer cannabis takers.

The law may act as a deterrent. It certainly makes pot smokers very secretive, but it would be optimistic to suppose that they give up taking cannabis as a result of an arrest.

The law is not an effective means of regulating private behaviour if there is too large a gulf between precept and practice. Many people in the United States were worried by the problem of alcohol and the prohibition of all drinks was seen as the answer. After a short period it was found that the experimental cure was worse than the ailment. The prohibition of off-course betting in this country had to be abandoned for similar reasons.

Some people have suggested that the clients of prostitutes, as well as the girls themselves, should be subject to the criminal law. But if the attempt to patronize a prostitute were made a crime, it would cause more social disruption than the harm caused by the evils of prostitution. Likewise it would be to the detriment of the whole community if all homosexuals were thrown into jail because most of them participate in the basic activities of society, in business, commerce, government, and the home.

In an earlier section of this chapter the law is criticized because it is unworkable. But if in fact it was made to work, the whole community would be disrupted. Hundreds of students would have to give up their studies, hundreds of young people would lose their jobs and hundreds more become social outcasts. This does not happen because most people who use cannabis go undetected. But a law which is tolerated only because it is unworkable, and which would cause chaos of it could be made effective, is plainly not a good law.

Many people now accept that the law should not try to regulate private behaviour (Hart, 1963). At one time blasphemy was punished, but now the police only make arrests when it is likely to cause a breach of the peace; attempted suicide is no longer a crime, although it is still forbidden by most religions; private homosexual acts are now not criminal although church dignitaries persist in calling them sinful. The laws on abortion, divorce and Sunday entertainment have recently been reformed.

There is a general feeling that nowadays there is too much legislation; unless the consequences are obviously and demonstrably harmful, it is wiser to permit than to repress. The permissive society has its drawbacks, but the repressive society has many more.

15   Legal, Medical and Social Controls

For and Against

Although this is not quite the end of the book, it is a convenient place to sum up the case for and against cannabis. No doubt many readers by now will view the author as a biased source of information. It may seem cavalier to reject the powerful body of opinion built up against cannabis over the last fifty years and to dismiss over a hundred articles describing the dangers of this drug.

The fact is that nearly all serious observers now agree that the case against cannabis is weak. All drugs have side effects of some kind. It is clear that in the short term the effects of cannabis are benign even when compared with some well-known drugs in everyday use, such as aspirin or penicillin.

Of course we cannot be absolutely sure of the long-term effects because the widespread use of cannabis is a recent phenomenon in this country. We have before us the awful warning of tobacco which is now known to be very harmful although for many years it was thought to be a mild drug. Certainly it is not beyond the bounds of possibility that cannabis will turn out to be equally harmful, but this argument is not by itself sufficient reason to ban it. The same argument could be used against all the recent medical discoveries which continue to be used very successfully against physical and mental ill-health.

I need less than a paragraph to answer the question: what will happen to you if you smoke pot? I can tell you for sure that you will not become addicted to it; you will not require increasing amounts to get the same effect; you will not produce monster children; you may find the experience rewarding or you may be quite disappointed with the effects. Whatever your background and predispositions may be, if you take cannabis, you are not more likely to commit other crimes; you are not more likely to escalate to more dangerous drugs; you are not more likely to have a mental breakdown; you are not more likely to become a layabout. The one serious thing that may happen to you is that you may get arrested and disgraced.

The arguments against the drug cannabis may not be compelling, but that is not to say that the case against the pot smoker is weak, or the opposition to legalization is misguided. Although there is now a very large number of people who use cannabis and this includes a wide variety of personality types, they all have one thing in common: they are all prepared to break the law in order to get a little extra pleasure. There are other reasons, such as fashion, a gesture of non-conformism, or social defiance; all these suggest that some pot smokers are attracted to the idea because it is illicit. Whether the user of cannabis seeks pleasure or the thrill of legal transgression, he is to be distinguished from the many other people who are now convinced that the sporadic use of cannabis is not irrevocably harmful, but who do not smoke pot because they do not wish to break the law. It would be a mistake to make too much of this, but it is reasonable to suppose that among the total group of all pot smokers, one would expect to find more than the average proportion of the irresponsible, and less than the average proportion of the responsible.

I have suggested earlier that it is neither wrong nor sinful to seek pleasure for its own sake. But this requires some qualification. If several hours of every week are devoted to the quiet and sedentary enjoyment of cannabis, then the user can be accused of self-indulgence and, even though he is not harming himself or society, he may be failing to reach his true potential.

These are not criticisms of the drug, but of the way it may be misused. Most of the problems of cannabis do not depend upon the drug *per se*, but upon the character and temperament of the users as well as the social setting. Doctors and social workers see and tend to write about the casualties of the drug scene, but this may give a misleading picture. The number of cannabis smokers who become casualties is probably very small, but their existence must be taken into account when weighing the balance for and against cannabis.

Legalization and Control

Many people will argue that cannabis is not a harmful drug, but legal controls are necessary. One important reason is that Britain is a party to the 1961 Single Convention on Narcotic Drugs. Although any party may denounce this treaty after six months' notice, this would seriously weaken the international control of opium. It would be possible for Britain to propose amendments, but it is very unlikely that any relaxation of the control of cannabis would be acceptable to most of the other nations.

Legalization would bring many technical problems which are far from solved. Certain essential safeguards would have to be devised if the transition from illegal blackmarket commodity to legal drug were to be made without confusion. The adulteration of cannabis would provide a difficult problem and standards of inspection would have to be agreed upon. It might |be possible to make a pure form of cannabis available through a Government-controlled agency as other countries have done with tobacco. This would create political problems, even though cannabis could become a useful source of revenue for the Exchequer.

The development of synthetic cannabis would make it easier to prevent adulteration and solve the difficult problem of sources of supply. It would be impossible for the Government to allow supplies to be obtained from countries where cannabis was still illegal. But there would have to be a licensing system for manufacturing synthetics.

Distribution would be difficult. Many people would object if cannabis were sold by the large tobacco combines or the drug houses, many of which are American satellites. On the other hand Government distribution, sold through the Post Office or at the Town Hall, seems an unlikely solution. Decisions would have to be made about the extent of advertising, if any were to be allowed at all. Would there be different brands of varying potency?

It would be necessary to devise a system similar to the breath-alyzer so that the amount in the body could be detected. Further-more, permitted limits of intoxication would have to be fixed; this proved to be a hard enough task with alcohol, but it would be still more difficult to obtain agreement when the drug is not so well known.

There would also have to be special measures to protect minors. This is particularly important with cannabis because it has such a powerful attraction for young people. It would be absurd to set the age limit too high, especially as the age for voting, marriage, con-tracts, etc., has just been lowered. On the other hand, adolescence is a time of stress and there is the danger that cannabis would be taken by immature users to avoid facing the many problems of growing up into adulthood. It would be difficult to choose the right age of consent and still more difficult to enforce this choice.

Finally it is clear that the public is not yet ready for the legaliza-tion of cannabis and would not accept the social changes it would bring. This, of course, is the strongest argument of all against making cannabis legally available.

Thus the legalization of cannabis would raise very difficult and complex problems which have not been given much thought, even by those who parade the streets with their 'Legalize Pot' slogans. This does not mean it is not a possibility in the future, perhaps before very long. But most people would agree that cannabis must be controlled at present.

But legal control is not the only possible approach. It is becoming clear that the law on cannabis is not a very effective deterrent, therefore it is a good idea to try some other method. One possibility is social control.

In the early years of an individual's life, social controls affect his behaviour through the use of power and discipline. Certain things are allowed and rewarded, other behaviour is disallowed and punished. Gradually the application of these sanctions becomes less necessary as the individual learns that certain things are 'done' and other things are 'not done'. Eventually these distinctions become part of his life style so that some forms of behaviour are acceptable and other activities are distasteful. This is what is meant when a person says that a particular activity is against his conscience – such behaviour makes him uncomfortable because it does not fit in with his image of himself, and therefore he does not engage in such behaviour.

There are already powerful social controls against drug taking and these could be developed and strengthened if supported by logical reasoning. Unfortunately the present social controls are collapsing because they are seen to be founded on misconceptions and misinformation. Nevertheless it is not difficult to make out a strong case for other forms of activity that are more interesting and more rewarding than the use of recreational drugs, and this is the kind of social control that would prove successful. The attractions of cannabis are relative. If you have something better to do, you are unlikely to want to take it.

Few people are impressed by this argument. Instead of legal control, the enlightened liberal is likely to advocate medical control. 'If you want to smoke pot, you must be sick, you poor boy.' Unfortunately there are serious disadvantages in this approach.

The Sickness Theory

Many humane and tolerant people are now suggesting that the drug user should be treated as a sick person rather than as a criminal. This is part of an increasingly prevalent tendency to regard non-conformity and mental illness as synonymous. But if taking cannabis is a psychological disorder, then it must be one of the most common forms of mental illness known to medicine. It would be an illness from which many thousands of men and women are suffering and would constitute as big a health problem as schizophrenia.

The reclassification of a certain type of behaviour as a disease rather than a sin or crime is sometimes a step towards a more enlightened approach, like the change of attitude towards madness (once regarded as possession by an evil spirit) or alcoholism (a matter solely for the police until recently). But medical history is full of mistakes and superstitions, like the 'toxicity' of menstruating women or the harmfulness of masturbation. Pot smoking as a clinical entity does not exist; to describe it as a sickness is to use the term to disguise moral disapproval.

Those who think of smoking pot as an illness will look for some predisposing psychological trait that explains why these sick men and women have turned to cannabis. But the motives for smoking pot are so varied, the social situations in which it is taken are so multifarious, and the manifested forms of behaviour are so heterogeneous, that it is difficult to believe that one trait will ever provide a satisfactory explanation. It is a bit like saying there is only one reason why some people like a bottle of wine with their dinner, why others like to spend an evening at the local, and why others need a stiff drink soon after they get up in the morning.

An essential component of the medical approach to cannabis is that it is undesirable and that the patient is cured only when he stops using it. Although the doctor prescribes drugs for most of his patients, he makes a sharp distinction between medicines like sedatives, tranquillizers and anti-depressants which are used to diminish emotional tension, and between recreational drugs like cannabis which he regards as non-therapeutic. The doctor regards the user of cannabis as someone who is anxious to escape from realities, but the pot smoker would claim that this is the drug that increases sensitivity and awareness.

The medical profession do not know what treatment to give to the pot smoker and the success rate of 'cures' is very low indeed. From the start the psychiatric situation is unpromising. The doctor is not part of his patient's world; he talks to him in a segregated setting at intervals of several days. Yet the psychiatrist's task is to counteract the influences that work continuously and pervasively when the patient is with his trusted friends. Even with a very competent and skilful psychiatrist, there are severe limitations to this type of approach. The only medical solution that stands much chance of being successful is to keep the pot smoker in an institution away from his drug. Thus the social consequences of regarding cannabis as a sickness are similar to that of viewing it as a sign of criminality.

The idea persists that no one would use cannabis if there were not something wrong with him. But people who hold this view usually have a particular type of cannabis user in mind. They are thinking of the young people wearing unusual clothes who have opted out of conventional society. The use of medical controls in these cases makes me suspect that it is not cannabis that we are trying to control, but a whole life-style involving other kinds of behaviour as well.

Similarities with Homosexuality

It is surprising how many similarities there are between the social problems of cannabis and homosexuality. Since the 1967 Sexual Offences Act homosexuals have a measure of freedom so that private acts are no longer criminal, but they are still regarded as medical cases and they still have legal and social restrictions compared with other people in the community. The Table on the following page summarizes the many similar situations that arise when confronted with the two types of behaviour, both subject to social disapproval although both are victimless crimes.

Both groups are thought to be something they are not. Both suffer from myths built up over the years. The information about both groups has been obtained from those who were arrested or were attending clincs, whereas the more typical homosexuals or pot smokers manage to avoid trouble. Both are thought to be sick and in need of medical attention. Many young people go through an adolescent phase of homosexuality and then develop an interest in the opposite sex, and many smoke pot on a few occasions and then give it up; but if either group are apprehended at this stage, they become known as perverts or drug addicts. Both groups have been the object of special campaigns by police, press and public. As this social hostility develops, both groups tend to form their exclusive coteries and lose contact with the dominant majority. Homosexual law reform was delayed for many years because any liberalization of the law was said to be condoning sexual laxity, and it was a brave MP who spoke up for homosexuals fifteen years ago; the same situation has now arisen with cannabis and very few MPs dare speak openly in favour of cannabis law reform.

The recent history of homosexual law reform may show how

Homosexuality	Cannabis
Indiscrimination	
Confused with child molesters	Confused with heroin addicts
Myths	
Untrustworthy	Criminals and assassins
Will proselytize	Escalate to hard drugs
Effeminate	Layabouts
Fall of Sodom and Gomorrah	Degradation and debauchery
Misinformation	
Reports based on those in prisons and clinics	Reports based on those arrested and deprived
Sickness Theory	
Ill and need to be cured	Ill and need to be cured
A Phase for Many	
But once caught known as a pervert	Once arrested known as a drug addict
Police Campaigns	
Special drives by vice squads	Special drug squads
Introverted Minority Groups	
Tendency to form coteries	Tendency to form coteries
Social hostility increases	Social hostility increases
Sub-culture develops	Sub-culture develops
Law Reform Delayed	
Appears to condone deviance	Appears to condone deviance
Politically inexpedient	Politically inexpedient

public attitudes to cannabis might change. At first ignorance about homosexuality was almost universal outside the ranks of homosexuals themselves; papers in the medical journals were as inaccurate and misinformed as the reports about cannabis. Very gradually knowledge was spread, usually from a special report (e.g. Westwood, 1952) or when a well-known person was arrested on a homosexual charge. Then the subject began to be mentioned and discussed. At last the issue was raised publicly and a special committee of inquiry was appointed to study the problem. Eventually the cautious recommendations of the committee were incorporated into an Act of Parliament.

Homosexual acts between consenting adults were made legal ten years after the Wolfenden report was published. How many years following the Wootton report will it be before these recommendations are made into law? It is to be hoped that the time lag will not be so long because already both the Wolfenden and the Wootton reports appear to be only a very cautious step forward.

The Concept of Deviance

Sociologists use the word deviance to describe behaviour which provokes social hostility. It is not the actual behaviour of the individual that makes a person deviant, but the reactions of others to that behaviour. Although homosexuals do not harm themselves or others, they are thought of as deviant because many people find their activities distasteful. The same might be said of gypsies. A child who is brought up in a loving home by two parents who are not married is a deviant; his upbringing and personality may be unexceptional, but his illegitimacy will become a social handicap as he grows older.

By the same criterion pot smoking is deviant. The effects of cannabis are insignificant, but the social hostility to using pot will have considerable effect on the smoker.

Deviance is one of the social controls discussed in the second part of this chapter. Social controls are part of civilized living, more efficient and less costly than legal controls. Ideally the degree of tolerance should depend upon the amount of social harm;

activities which have a disruptive influence should be limited by
strong social controls, while socially harmless activities should be
uncontrolled. Unfortunately this is not always the case. Motoring
offences do not arouse much disapproval although they are poten-
tially very harmful. On the other hand ideas of right and wrong as
regards sexual behaviour have always been the subject of strong
convictions without reference to their social effects.

Sometimes the social standards are found to be out of date
because conditions have changed and new information has become
available. In such an event it is quite difficult to change these social
standards.

New knowledge may show that the social controls are too weak.
A case could be made in favour of having stronger social controls
against smoking tobacco or getting slightly drunk. At other times
the new knowledge suggests that the social controls are unnecessarily strong. Dancing on Sundays, gambling, abortion, the censor-
ship of books and plays, are all examples of where our social
standards have been relaxed. Perhaps the use of cannabis is an
example of a social control that is unnecessarily strong. When
there is doubt and controversy, the will of the majority is often
enforced by strength and power, not by discussion and reason.

Scapegoats and Witch hunts

By now it will be clear that difficulties are caused, not only by the
effects of cannabis and by the personality of the user, but in a
large measure by the attitude of non-users to those who take pot.
This is nothing new. Throughout history the dominant majority
has sought out and punished convenient scapegoats.

If the age-old idea of the scapegoat were true and we really could
cure some of the ills of our society by sacrificing a few individuals,
there might be something to be said for it and the only difficulty
would be to decide who is to be next. But the sacrifice does not
decrease our troubles. It increases them. Not only is it unjust and
cruel to the goat, it covers up the problems instead of solving them.
The scapegoat's punishment deflects the same fate from us for the
sins we have committed ourselves. At the same time the scapegoat

provides us with the flattering illusion that we are superior to him (Taylor and Rey, 1953). In recent years the user of cannabis has been used as a convenient scapegoat and has been persecuted with a vindictiveness that is not related to the harm he has caused, but rather to the mythical magnitude of his wickedness.

There are signs that we have at last reached the lowest point of the drug scare and there will now be some improvement as the witch hunt dies. (Who will be the next scapegoat?) The rational arguments in the Wootton report will convince some people, while others will react against the reception of the report in Parliament. Even the new Government legislation acknowledges that cannabis use is not the same thing as heroin addiction. Some magistrates are now giving less severe sentences and probation officers have shown a sensible awareness of the difficulties. The work of the people at Release and in other organizations of the underground is beginning to have some effect.

But there is a long way to go. I meet many wonderful people whose life is spent in the service of others, dedicated to social welfare, taking away misery and adding to the sum of human happiness. And yet if someone uses a chemical crutch to find his own deeper more private happiness, these well-intentioned people are horrified. They will do everything they can to prevent the use of cannabis, assuming that the user will only hurt himself and end up on the scrap heap like the meths drinker. Of course it is inevitable that some will misuse drugs, including cannabis, but many will not. But even when we know a person is misusing a drug, we should hesitate before we arrest him and lock him up.

The New Attitude to Drugs

There are several reasons why many people have turned against the traditional recreational drug of alcohol and prefer to use cannabis. One important reason is that we now live in a society where many different types of drugs are used and accepted. The most typical drug addict in this country is a woman of about fifty who is taking sleeping pills every night and tranquillizers every day; she would not for a moment think she was anything but normal because many of her friends are doing the same. In a three-year period forty-three million prescriptions were issued to National Health Service patients for sleeping pills, tranquillizers, slimming pills, anti-depressants and stimulants. Others take regular daily doses of aspirins or other medicines for which a prescription is not needed; most of these are dangerous except when taken in very small quantities. The man who spends pounds a week which he can ill afford on cigarettes which are harmful to his health is seriously addicted.

Drugs are taken by depressed housewives, by businessmen to pep them up at important conferences, by soldiers to put off exhaustion, and by sportsmen of all kinds. It is well known that professional cyclists use amphetamines; similar drugs are used in boxing, football, tennis and rowing. Marksmen and archers use sedatives to steady their hands and rally drivers use stimulants to keep them awake. There is open discussion on TV about the drugs taken by astronauts on a space mission. Children who grow up in this environment are much more likely to turn to drugs to help them solve a problem or relax for a few hours.

Another reason for the increase in the use of cannabis is the growth of the misnamed permissive society. There has been a growing emphasis on the cultivation of aesthetic and mildly hedonistic sensibilities. This is in line with current economic trends. Before long working hours will become shorter and less important. The old puritan ethic which glorified work for its own sake will be less meaningful and leisure activities will become more important. There will then be time to enjoy more than the usual superficial pleasures and special efforts will be made to appreciate good music, art, food and sex. In such an atmosphere the boundaries of permissible pleasure are extended and experimentation is encouraged. The use of cannabis to produce new sensory stimulation is a logical development of this ethic.

The Attitude of the Young

Although it is possible to exaggerate the extent to which cannabis is used by young people, the drug is fast becoming part of the teenage mythology. This does not imply that most teenagers smoke pot; many do not wish to, but they nevertheless are prepared to defend their friends who do; others have tried it and decided it is not for them, although many of their friends take cannabis. Although youth is said to be in revolt against conventional behaviour, there is strong conformism among young people as can be observed by their dress, hair styles, preferences in music. Tolerance towards cannabis is one of the accepted attitudes.

One of the strongest influences on a teenager's behaviour in any sphere is what other teenagers are thinking and doing and the desire to be like them. In the past young people were most influenced by adult groups in close proximity – their family, their neighbours, their workmates. Now the most influential factor is a separate teenage mythology. Aspirations must fit in with this image of the typical teenager, and young people who cannot measure up to the archetype begin to feel either that they are missing something, or that something is missing in them.

In an earlier research (Schofield, 1968) I noted the power of this teenage mythology and the way it influenced sexual behaviour. If the individual regarded himself as part of the youth scene, his attitude to premarital sexual intercourse was much more tolerant. The same situation applies to teenage attitudes to cannabis. Of course attitudes influence behaviour, so pot smoking is much more common among boys and girls who regard themselves as part of the teenage scene.

Young people are very mobile. Not long ago a youth craze was often confined to one area or social class. The teenage mythology is international and classless. So it was inevitable that cannabis would spread quickly from the ports and large urban areas. Today there are many small towns where cannabis coteries have been established.

Young people have always tended to be idealistic and hence anti-materialist; a good job, a nice house and material possessions have only become pressing objectives after getting married and starting a family. The difference today is that the limitations of a predominantly materialist way of life have become clearer, and many young people want more out of life than a routine job, a television and a washing machine. And they really do shudder at leading the same kind of lives as their parents. Some adolescents start drinking so as to be thought grown up like their parents, whereas others take drugs in order to be different from their parents.

But when they revolt against the conventional lives of older generations and proclaim their right to do their own thing, they are not thinking of an anarchic free-for-all. Their own thing is a meditative realization of their own senses and a greater awareness of their inner self. Many of them claim that cannabis helps them to achieve this quasi-religious state, and they can cite historical support for this claim, for the Indian priests have used cannabis to help them in their religious meditations for hundreds of years.

Youthful experiments are part of growing up; young people need the opportunity to stretch their minds as well as their bodies. There must be limits, but they should be as wide as possible. One possible attitude is that it doesn't matter what you do as long as you don't harm others or do yourself a permanent injury.

Certain young people carry their experiments beyond a protest against the life styles of their parents. Their dissent is against the basic structure of the society in which they find themselves and by which they feel trapped. Visible signs are necessary to register their dissent, but the present young generation usually prefers a non-violent form of protest. So they organize demonstrations to uphold unpopular causes and openly defy conventional rules by wearing unusual clothes, by adopting a relaxed attitude to sex, and by taking cannabis.

This is very disturbing for the older generations because it is unlike the traditional sowing of wild oats which is essentially transitory. This is a movement which seeks to have permanent consequences. It is a youthful revolt that we should take seriously. Exasperating thought it may be, it is not an unhealthy phase for the young people concerned, providing they eventually find values and standards that they can accept with some sort of contentment. Nor is it unhealthy for the community which can profit from these new and stimulating elements. The progress of society depends upon the conflict between the youthful activists and the defenders of the status quo. It is possible that our urgent desire to suppress the use of cannabis is confused with our alarm at the way the young challenge our social and political views.

The Ideal Recreational Drug

Of course there is no such thing as an ideal recreational drug at present. Cannabis like every other legal or illegal drug falls far short of the ideal. The pro-pot lobby has tended to oversell the advantages of pot with dreamy descriptions of getting high and self-admiring talk about the lovely people who take it. It is a mistake to claim too much for cannabis, for there are several drawbacks.

Its effects are unpredictable and its action imprecise. For many it does not work at all, and for others its effects are variable. It depends too much upon the mood of the user at the time he takes it. Regular users say it does not help them when they are depressed. An antagonistic person in the cannabis circle can spoil it for others. A few people have had a frightening experience while under the

influence of cannabis – nothing like so severe as a bad trip with
LSD but unpleasant enough at the time.

The ideal recreational drug would make us feel relaxed and
happy and act as a social lubricant. It would not give rise to physical or psychological dependence and it would have no undesirable
side effects. Soma, the fictional drug in Aldous Huxley's *Brave
New World* gave great pleasure harmlessly. 'One cubic centimetre
cures ten gloomy sentiments,' said the Assistant Predestinator.

You would need a whole range of such drugs, each of which
would do exactly what is wanted, to the degree wanted. One drug
to stimulate us to action and make us more efficient at work or
play; another to calm us down and allow us to feel amiable at
home; another to produce geniality and help us to be cheerful with
our friends; and another to send us happily to sleep.

The pharmaceutical revolution in drugs working on the central
nervous system may turn this fantasy into a reality within the next
decade or so. Knowledge of how the brain works is increasing
rapidly and soon a new group of drugs will be discovered that will
influence human sensations and moods by acting on basic cerebral
mechanisms.

If a harmless recreational drug were produced tomorrow, would
we welcome it, or would we try to ban it? Writers of fiction are not
optimistic about the consequences of such a discovery. Soma was
given to the citizens of *Brave New World* to keep them quiet and
stifle opposition. In the *Space Merchants*, a novel by Frederick
Pohl and C. M. Kornbluth, a firm gives away free samples of its
latest drink, Coffiest, which contains a safe drug; it is so delicious
that people become hooked on it and are Coffiest customers for
life. In *What Shall We Do Till The Analyst Comes*, another story
by Frederick Pohl, a harmless drug called Cheery-Gum is so re-
laxing that people chew it continually and no longer bother to
work.

When the ideal recreational drug appears in the real world perhaps it will not be exploited by the Government or commercial
interests, but it will probably be forbidden by a zealous Home
Secretary of the future. This is because ignorance breeds fear. We
have not come to terms with the idea of recreational drugs and so

we cannot start to think out our attitudes towards chemical aids to pleasure. Until we have developed a social philosophy, we are unable to make intelligent judgements about their use and abuse.

A Social Philosophy for Drugs

The only identifiable philosophy at present is a mixture of revulsion, incomprehension, fascination, and a vague feeling that the doctors should tell us which drugs should be legal and which should be outlawed. In fact it is impossible to get any kind of consensus from the medical profession and each doctor vigorously claims the right to prescribe whatever drug he fancies. Yet it is now believed that less than a dozen misguided doctors started the heroin epidemic and most medical men will admit that there is a vast amount of irresponsible over-prescribing of drugs in their profession. In fact it is unreasonable to expect busy family doctors to make decisions about drugs and social policy. In any case the average doctor knows very little about cannabis, for he never prescribes it, and his patients do not ask him to cure them of pot smoking.

As in all kinds of health education, it is always difficult to know how far one should go when trying to stop people from doing something which is harmful. It is particularly difficult when there is a long interval between the act and the injury. If the consequences of smoking tobacco were to be seen in weeks instead of years, it is certain that many more people would give up cigarettes. But even then it would be hard to make out a case in favour of banning all cigarettes. It undoubtedly helps some people to concentrate and it relieves tension for others. When I gave up smoking, I promptly put on thirty pounds and fat people are much more likely to suffer from hardening of the arteries, blood clots and heart disease – all major causes of death in this country. In any case an attempt to ban cigarettes would fail. Too many people are dependent on tobacco and it has become associated with many other pleasant activities in our daily lives.

We should accept the fact that some people need a chemical crutch to help them through each day. There are morphine addicts who continue to work and there are others leading useful lives although the daily supply of tablets had become an indispensable part of their way of life, just as there are successful alcoholics. Only those who never take tea, coffee or a coke and put no nutmeg in their puddings are in a position to criticize.

A feasible social philosophy for a recreational drug would start by accepting that a minority wants to use it: in a free and tolerant society they should be allowed to do so unless it can be conclusively shown that they will harm themselves or the community: the onus of proof is on those who wish to prohibit the drug altogether: but even though it seems unlikely that there are any long-term unpleasant physical or psychological effects, we cannot always be sure; there may also be unexpected social disadvantages if the drug becomes freely available without further study: for these reasons we do not wish to encourage people to take it, therefore commercial exploitation should be forbidden and public demand should not be artificially stimulated: so the use of a recreational drug must be controlled in some way. The extent of this control is a matter for debate.

The Legal Control of Cannabis

If you cannot accept the social philosophy suggested in the previous paragraph as appropriate for cannabis, the alternatives are:
to make it available immediately without restrictions;
to sell it under license with restrictions on quality, potency and distribution;
to exercise a measure of control by taxation, as we do with alcohol and tobacco;
to control it medically by letting each doctor decide who shall have it and who shall not;
to suppress it with the full force of the law, including stiffer penalties and increased police activity;
or to leave things as they are.

No doubt this last suggestion will be most popular. Social researchers (Schofield, 1969) have found that there is a strong predisposition in favour of the legal status quo and opposition to almost any change in the law; attitudes to a particular issue are obscured by the sanctity of the law and opposition to reform only subsides after the law has been changed.

In a country well known for its devotion to traditional ways and its instinctive reluctance to change, there are bound to be other more urgent reforms. It would be hard to make out a convincing case for the early legalization of cannabis when there are other more important things to be done. One cannot say, as one could say about the pressing problem of birth control and the rising world population, that we will all suffer if we do not act quickly. Nevertheless while the law stands as it does, injustices are being done in our name.

The difficulty with the present law on cannabis is that it raises all the problems usually encountered with laws that seek to control private behaviour. In the previous chapter I defined deviance as an element which is not inherent in the behaviour itself, but which is the result of an attitude conferred upon the behaviour. Despite the absence of a victim or damage to the interests of others, behaviour designated as deviant usually attracts legal sanctions. In effect this is moral intervention – an attempt to outlaw immorality. The difficulty is that one man's moral turpitude is another man's innocent pleasure.

Inevitably laws that are concerned with private activities are an interference with our freedom, and they pose a still more serious threat for there is only a slight difference between the control of moral behaviour and thought reform or brain washing. Such laws can only be enforced by resorting to doubtful police methods and by accepting rough justice. Taking a single puff of a joint does not make an individual part of the drug scene, but it does make him liable to arrest and punishment.[1]

As public opinion cannot be ignored, my own suggestion is an interim change in the law, to be reviewed in three years. I should like to see a more sophisticated law in which the seriousness of

---

1. It might be said that it requires rather less than a single puff to lead to arrest; when cannabis is found by the police on premises, it has usually been concealed in a hiding place, so that it may easily happen that it does not in truth belong to the person who has been arrested.

the offence would be measured by the quantity found in the individual's possession. Thus the difference between possession for private use and possession for dealing would be written into the law. Accordingly I suggest:

(1) Possession of up to 30 grams of cannabis should be a summary offence only, punishable on a first or subsequent conviction by a maximum fine of £20.

(2) Possession of any amount larger than 30 grams should be punishable (*a*) on summary conviction by a fine not exceeding £100 or imprisonment of a term not exceeding four months; (*b*) on conviction of indictment by an unlimited fine or imprisonment for a term not exceeding two years or both.

(3) The procedure on indictment should be subject to the Attorney-General's approval.

(4) The police powers to stop and search without a warrant should be withdrawn.

If these recommendations were adopted, no international treaty would be broken, because the 1961 Single Convention only requires 'imprisonment or other penalties of deprivation of liberty' for 'serious offences'. The first two recommendations would make it more difficult for the supplier of cannabis. The users would wish to buy in amounts of less than 30 grams and so the supplier would have to make more sales. A substantial amount of the smuggling of cannabis is already in small amounts and is not exploited to any significant extent by professional criminals. If this quantitative formula were introduced, dealings in cannabis would become still less attractive to organized crime. The profit to be made on 30 grams of cannabis is not enough to attract big-time crooks.

I have suggested that the supplies of cannabis should be made more difficult to obtain, not because I believe in the myth of the wicked pusher as the framers of the new Government legislation seem to, but because this measure will slow down the spread of cannabis to new users, thereby giving us time to contain the situation until we learn more about it.

Nevertheless it is meant to indicate that the use of cannabis is not a serious offence and for this reason the powers of the police should be strictly limited. In addition to the withdrawal of the police powers of stop and search, I hope other measures will be taken against malpractices brought to light by evidence put before the Deedes sub-committee. Their report was disappointing and negative because four members were determined to resist any change; as they repeatedly stated in committee, the drug problem is so serious that the police should be given maximum powers and should not be restricted. But this is an attitude that needs to be qualified.

There is not one drug problem, but several, and it is a mistake to confuse them. Most people would agree a very serious problem is created by those who inject heroin or other drugs intravenously. But the importance of cannabis was under-emphasized in the Deedes report. An analysis of all drug offences has shown that most people are convicted for possessing small amounts of cannabis. There must be some doubt whether such wide police powers are justified for an offence which the Advisory Committee on Drug Dependence has recommended 'should not normally be regarded as a serious crime to be punished by imprisonment'.

Although it is often alleged that it is difficult to consider police powers in relation to cannabis alone, at least the law should make this distinction, even if it cannot be put into practice on every occasion. No doubt there are times when the police search for one drug and find another. But there are other occasions when the reasonable grounds for suspicion can relate only to the suspected use of cannabis. The distinction between cannabis and more harmful drugs can and should also be made with regard to other laws and administrative regulations (e.g. applications for search warrants, granting bail).

So in effect the use of cannabis in private homes would not be subject to legal interference and consenting adults smoking in private would not be harassed by the police. This may seem to be advocating a contradictory position – it is wrong to legalize cannabis but right to treat individual cases of pot smoking as relatively trivial offences. The contradiction is unavoidable in the present state of public opinion. Indeed it reflects the contradictions in society itself, with its indifference to the harmfulness of socially accepted drugs like alcohol and tobacco, its deep suspicion of social innovations by the young, and its confusion between the really dangerous drugs and the relatively mild effects of cannabis.

This limited change in the law would provide time for the public to readjust to the new information about cannabis. After having been told for many years that cannabis is an unmitigated social evil, it will be some time before people can forget the misinformation and scare tactics of the past and accept the recent reappraisal of this drug.

Meanwhile much work would have to be done during the three-year interim period. The international organizations would have to be told of our new approach to the problem and attempts made to renegotiate the treaty, for no country should opt out of the international control of narcotics, if this can be avoided.

Everyone agrees that further research on the long-term effects is necessary and this should be started immediately because there must be an inquiry into the social effects, which inevitably takes a long time. Some people talk as if research is a magic wand that will cure all our ills, and politicians sometimes suggest waiting for research results because it puts off the problem for a few more years. But despite the many reports on the pharmacology of cannabis, there has been hardly any social research on the prevalence and effects of regular usage in this country.

No one can forecast the results of this research, but the evidence suggests that, as the years go by, the controls on cannabis will become progressively less strict. Therefore it would be useful to use this interim period to conduct an exhaustive study of the practical problems of legalization, so as to be ready to meet the difficulties of transition, safeguards, adulteration, standards, distribution and other problems noted in chapter 15.

A final task during this interim period would be to take a long look at our legal administrative procedures from the moment a person is arrested for possessing an illegal drug to the time he has served his sentence or paid the penalty. Most people would agree that the law should be concerned with the more dangerous drugs like heroin. But it should look less like a vast boot intent on stamping out a social evil, and more like a community net designed to catch the multiple-drug taker before he sinks too far beyond help. Whatever sanctions it may be necessary to write into the law, there would be much to be gained if the police thought of themselves as an agency primarily concerned with discovering the addict and passing him on to those who can help him.

So What Shall We Do?

The new law, as proposed at present, will not make much difference to the user of cannabis and will solve none of the problems. For those who are not content with the existing unsatisfactory situation, action is required in six areas.

(1) Work towards a more sensible law.
(2) Call for more vigorous research.
(3) Accept that we now live in a drug-orientated society.
(4) Provide better education.
(5) Insist upon the individual's right to choose.
(6) Reduce the emotional impact.

Some people may think that law reform may not be necessary because the police might lose interest in arresting pot smokers if magistrates give out smaller sentences. But a change of opinion does not always precede a reform of the law. Sometimes attitudes await a change in the law. A more tolerant attitude to homosexuality followed after the 1967 Sexual Offences Act and the laws against racial prejudice are justified because they will affect public opinion even though they are difficult to enforce in practice.

As a new generation comes into Parliament there is bound to be a change of attitude and probably a higher proportion of Members will have tried cannabis. In the days when homosexuality was frequently debated in the house, there was always gossip that certain MPs were homosexual; it was impossible to verify these rumours and it was noticeable that those who were alleged to be homosexual were not forward in advocating law reform. Today one hears similar rumours about Members of Parliament who smoke pot; it is just as difficult to verify these rumours and certainly none of them have given any outward sign of support for cannabis law reform.

But as the use of cannabis seems to be spreading throughout all social strata of the population, it is inevitable that more and more politicians, lawyers, doctors, teachers and others with influence will be pot smokers. For all these reasons a campaign for a more enlightened law will not be a waste of time.

As people have been saying ever since the publication of the Wootton report, there must be more research, although there is little sign of progress. Perhaps it is a little unfortunate that Professor Paton, the leading critic of pot smoking, is both chairman of the important pharmacological working party of the Medical Research Council and chairman of the projects and publications committee of the Institute for the Study of Drug Dependence. Of the five social researches on cannabis known to the Home Office in 1970, three are by doctors who have already published papers describing cannabis as very harmful.

We must face the fact that drugs are now a part of our civilization. It is probably better to do without, if one can, because in the present state of our pharmacological knowledge, there are disadvantages and unpleasant aspects in all the drugs known to man. Ideally we should not take drugs, but such restraint would not be usual or normal. We have to abandon this assumption that an individual *ought* to be able to do without a recreational drug and that those who take them are immature, degraded, sick or criminal. It is not a question of stamping out all drug taking; such a campaign is doomed to failure now, even if it were ever possible. The question is how far recreational drugs need to be controlled, remembering that the best method of control is social, not legal, so that abstinence from drugs is a measure of character, just as it is with alcohol and tobacco.

The call for education is as inevitable as the demand for research, especially when dealing with an intractable problem. Education is often a disguised term for propaganda, consisting of a description of the harmful effects of the drug and the relevant law, in the hope that this will act as an effective deterrent. It is a vain hope because any pot smoker knows far more than the average non-user about the effects of the drug. But a gradual educational campaign is the only possible method in a free society when new knowledge reveals public ignorance. The general process of discussion and argument is the best method of public enlightenment and, slow though it may be, is the best way towards a balanced solution of a community problem.

Having produced the evidence, as far as we know it, the individual must be allowed to choose for himself, and no one should be very surprised if the choice is not firmly based on logic. As in every health education problem, this really is as far as we should go. It is often possible to find good reasons for restricting a person's freedom to choose so that we can minimize the potential harm he might do to himself. But unless the drawbacks far outweigh the advantages, each person should be free to make the wrong choice. As far as cannabis is concerned, it is up to the prohibitors to supply the damning evidence. Aside from the point that it is always more difficult to demonstrate a negative proposition (e.g. that something is not harmful), those who wish to ban cannabis must produce convincing reasons before we restrict the individual's right to choose.

Finally there is an urgent need to take some of the emotional steam out of the controversy. This applies to those in favour of pot smoking as well as those who are against it. The cannabis debate has given rise to so much moral indignation that it has begun to assume an exaggerated importance out of all proportion to its true significance.

Unfortunately the relative importance of a social problem depends not upon its disruptive influence, but upon the values attached to it by the people in the community. Sometimes this leads to badly distorted impressions of the social significance of a problem. Thus the problem of witchcraft in the Middle Ages was partly based upon a misjudgement of the power of the witches. Large modern societies consist of a variety of social groups within which a certain kind of behaviour is accepted; whereas the same behaviour would be considered strange outside the group. There are a large number of diverse groups or sub-cultures, each with its own patterns of behaviour and it is likely that almost everyone takes part in some behaviour which other people in the same society would think of as odd or unusual. But it is only when people start to disapprove actively that the behaviour becomes deviant and thus unacceptable.

It is possible that we are making too much of the problem of cannabis. Perhaps things would be better if we worried about it less. It would certainly be true to say that our efforts would be more fruitful if we sought to contain the problem by social controls, instead of trying to eliminate it with heavy legal sanctions.

No doubt this attitude will be attacked because it is too fatalistic. We live in an activist society where people believe that we can do almost anything if we try hard enough. Such an activist attitude is good, for it is the means of curbing previously unchecked diseases, reducing poverty, providing shelter for the homeless, and solving other social problems.

But this solid faith in our achievements sometimes results in an urgent desire to change someone who does not measure up to our expectations. The rights of each individual are more important than the effects of pot.

There is still a very large number of people who do not want to use cannabis, and in the future there will be a vast number who have tried it and decided not to go on using it. It is the sheer passivity of pot that makes it unattractive. There are so many other things to enjoy that sitting around introspectively smoking pot seems dull and empty.

But even if a large proportion of the new generation decide that cannabis is not for them, I believe they will be less upset by the problem and more tolerant towards those who want to use it. This is the attitude that will prevail in the end and, what is more, it is right.

References

ALLENTUCK, S., and BOWMAN, K. M., 'The Psychiatric Aspects of Marihuana Intoxication', *American Journal of Psychiatry*, vol. 99, 1942, p. 248.

ALLPORT, GORDON W., *The Nature of Prejudice*, Addison-Wesley, Reading, Mass., 1954.

ANSLINGER, HARRY J., 'Assassin of Youth', *The American Magazine*, vol. 124, July 1937, p. 18.

ANSLINGER, HARRY J., and TOMKINS, W. G., *The Traffic in Narcotics*, Funk & Wagnalls, New York, 1953.

ANSLINGER, HARRY J., and OURSLER, FULTON, *The Murderers*, Farrar, Strauss & Cudahy, New York, 1961.

AUSUBEL, DAVID P., *Drug Addiction: Physiological, Psychological and Sociological Aspects*, Random House, New York, 1964.

BECKER, HOWARD, *Outsiders*, The Free Press, New York, 1963.

BECKER, HOWARD, 'History, Culture and Subjective Experience: An Exploration of the Social Bases of Drug-Induced Experiences', *Journal of Health and Social Behaviour*, vol. 8, 1967, pp. 163–76.

BECKETT, DALE, 'Should We Legalize Pot?', *New Society*, 18 May 1967, pp. 720–21.

BENABUD, A., 'Psychopathological Aspects of the Cannabis Situation in Morocco; Statistical Data for 1956', *U.N. Bulletin on Narcotics*, vol. 9, no. 4, 1957, pp. 1–16.

BENDER, L., 'Drug Addiction in Adolescence', *Comprehensive Psychiatry*, vol. 4, 1963, pp. 181–94.

BEWLEY, T. H., 'Recent Changes in the Pattern of Drug Abuse in London and the U.K.', *British Medical Journal*, vol. 2, 1965, p. 1284.

BLOOMQUIST, E. R., *Marijuana*, Collier-MacMillan, 1968.

BLUM, RICHARD, *et al.*, *The Utopiates*, Tavistock, 1965.

BLUMER, HERBERT, et al., The World of Youthful Drug Use, University of California, Berkeley, 1967.

BOUQUET, J., 'Cannabis', U.N. Bulletin on Narcotics, vol. 3, no. 1, 1951, pp. 22–45.

BRICKMAN, H. R., 'The Psychedelic "Hip Scene": Return of the Death Instinct', American Journal of Psychiatry, vol. 125, 1968, p. 766.

BROMBERG, W., 'Marihuana Intoxication. A Clinical Study of Cannabis Sativa Intoxication', American Journal of Psychiatry, vol. 91, 1934, pp. 303–30.

BROMBERG, W., 'Marihuana: A Psychiatric Study', Journal of the American Medical Association, vol. 113, no. 1, 1939, pp. 4–12.

CHAPPLE, P. A. L., 'Cannabis: A Toxic and Dangerous Substance. A Study of 80 Takers', British Journal of Addiction, vol. 61, 1966, p. 269.

CHAREN, S., and PERELMAN, L., 'Personality Studies of Marihuana Addicts', American Journal of Psychiatry, vol. 102, 1946, p. 674.

CHEIN, ISIDOR, et al., Narcotics, Delinquency and Social Policy: The Road to H, Tavistock, 1964.

CHOPRA, R. N., and CHOPRA, I. C., 'Cannabis Sativa in Relation to Mental Disease and Crime in India', Indian Journal of Medical Research, vol. 30, 1942, pp. 155–71.

CHOPRA, R. N., and CHOPRA, G. S., 'Treatment of Drug Addiction; Experience in India', U.N. Bulletin on Narcotics, vol. 9, no. 4, 1957, pp. 21–33.

CHOPRA, R. N., and CHOPRA, I. C., Drug Addiction with Special Reference to India, Council of Scientific and Industrial Research, New Delhi, 1965.

CHRISTIANSEN, J., and RAFAELSEN, O. J., 'Cannabis Metabolites in Urine After Oral Administration', Psychopharmacologia, vol. 15, 1969, p. 60.

CLARK, KENNETH B., Dark Ghetto, Harper and Row, New York, 1965.

CONNELL, P. H., Amphetamine Psychosis, Chapman & Hall, 1958.

COON, CAROLINE, and HARRIS, RUFUS, The Release Report on Drug Offenders and the Law, Sphere, 1969.

CRANCER, ALFRED, et al. 'Comparison of the Effect of Marihuana and Alcohol on Simulated Driving Performance', Science, vol. 164, 1969, pp. 851–4.

DAWTRY, FRANK, (Ed.), Social Problems of Drug Abuse, Butterworths, 1968.

DOWNES, D. M., The Delinquent Solution, Routledge & Kegan Paul, 1966.

EBIN, DAVID, (Ed.), The Drug Experience, The Orion Press, New York, 1961.

References   197

EDDY, N., HALBACH, H., ISBELL, H., and SEEVERS, M., 'Drug Dependence: Its Significance and Characteristics', *Bulletin of the World Health Organization*, vol. 32, no. 5, 1965, pp. 721–33.

FREEDMAN, H. L., and ROCKMORE, M. J., 'Marihuana, Factor in Personality Evaluation and Army Maladjustment', *Journal of Clinical Psychopathology*, vols. 7 and 8, 1946, pp. 765–82 and 221–36.

GARATTINI, S., 'Effects of a Cannabis Extract on Gross Behaviour', in *Hashish: Its Chemistry and Pharmacology*, CIBA Foundation Study Group, 21, Churchill, 1965.

GARDIKAS, C. G., 'Hashish and Crime', *Eukephalas*, vol. 2–3, 1950, p. 203.

GAUTIER, THÉOPHILE, 'Le Club des Hachichins', *La Revue des Deux Mondes*, 1 February 1846.

GLATT, M. M., 'Drug Treatment Centres', *British Medical Journal*, vol. 3, 1967, p. 242.

GOMILA, F. R., and LAMBOU, M. C. G., in WALTON, R. P., (Ed.), *Marihuana: America's New Drug Problem*, Lippincott, Philadelphia, 1938.

GOODE, ERICH, (Ed.), *Marihuana*, Atherton Press, New York, 1969.

GOODE, ERICH, 'Marihuana and the Politics of Reality', *Journal of Health and Social Behaviour*, vol. 10, 1969, p. 83.

GOODMAN, L. S., and GILMAN, A., *The Pharmacological Basis of Therapeutics*, Macmillan, New York, 1965.

HANEVELD, G. T., 'Hashish in Lebanon', *Nederlandsch Tijdschritt voor Geneeskunde*, vol. 103, 1959, pp. 686–8.

HART, H. L. A., *Law, Liberty and Morality*, Oxford University Press, 1963.

HART, TOM, and NATION, R. N. N., 'Drug Taking Amongst Teenage Girls', in *The Anti-Social Child in Care*, Residential Child Care Association, 1966.

HINDMARCH, I., 'Drug Use in a Provincial University', *British Journal of Addiction*, vol. 64, 1970, p. 395.

HOLLISTER, L. E., RICHARDS, R. K., and GILLESPIE, H. K., 'Comparison of THC and Synhexyl in Man', *Clinical Pharmacological Therapeutics*, vol. 9, 1968, p. 782.

HUXLEY, ALDOUS, *The Doors of Perception*, Penguin, 1959.

ISBELL, H., et al., 'Effects of (—) delta 9 trans-tetrahydrocannabinol in Man', *Psychopharmacologia*, vol. 11, 1967, pp. 184–8.

JAMES, I. P., 'Delinquency and Heroin Addiction in Britain', *British Journal of Criminology*, vol. 9, no. 2, 1969, pp. 108–24.

JORGENSEN, F., 'Abuse of Psychtomimetics', *Acta Psychiatrica Scandinavica*, suppl. 203, 1968, p. 215.

References

KAPLAN, JOHN, *Marijuana – The New Prohibition*, World, New York, 1970.

KEELER, M. H., 'Adverse Reactions to Marihuana', *American Journal of Psychiatry*, vol. 124, 1967, p. 674.

KOLB, LAWRENCE, *Drug Addiction: A Medical Problem*, Thomas, Springfield, Illinois, 1962.

LAURIE, PETER, *Drugs: Medical, Psychological and Social Facts*, Penguin, 1969.

LEARY, TIMOTHY, *et al.*, *The Psychedelic Experience*, University Books, New York, 1964.

LEECH, K., and JORDON, B., *Drugs for Young People: Their Use and Misuse*, Religious Educational Press, 1967.

LEECH, K., *The Drug Subculture: A Christian Analysis*, Church Information Office, 1969.

LINDESMITH, ALFRED, *The Addict and the Law*, Indiana University Press, Bloomington, 1965.

LITTLE, KENNETH, *Negroes In Britain*, Routledge & Kegan Paul, 1947.

MANHIEMER, D. I., and MELLINGER, G. D., 'Marihuana Use Among Urban Adults', *Science*, vol. 166, 1969, p. 1,544.

MARCOVITZ, E.. 'Marihuana Problems', *Journal of the American Medical Association*, vol. 129, 1945, p. 378.

MATZA, D., *Becoming Deviant*, Prentice-Hall, New Jersey, 1969.

MAURER, D. W., and VOGEL, V. H., *Narcotics and Narcotic Addiction*, Thomas, Springfield, Illinois, 1967.

MCGLOTHLIN, WILLIAM, 'Hallucinogen Drugs: A Perspective with Special Reference to Cannabis' in SOLOMON, D., (Ed.), *The Marihuana Papers*, Signet, New York, 1968.

MILLER, DONALD, E., 'Narcotic Drug and Marijuana Controls' in *Background Papers on Student Drug Involvement*, U.S. National Student Association, Washington, 1967.

MILMAN, D. H., 'The Role of Marihuana in Patterns of Drug Abuse by Adolescents', *Journal of Pediatrics*, vol. 74, 1969, p. 283.

MIRAS, CONSTANTINOS, 'Some Aspects of Cannabis Action in *Hashish: Its Chemistry and Pharmacology*, CIBA Foundation Study Group, 21, Churchill, 1965.

MITCHELL, ALEX, 'Drugs is a 5 Letter Word', *OZ*, vol. 22, July 1969, pp. 22–3.

MORAES ANDRADE, O., 'The Criminogenic Action of Cannabis (marihuana) and Narcotics', *U.N. Bulletin on Narcotics*, vol. 16, no. 4, 1964, pp. 23–8.

MOREAU, J., 'Lypemanie avec Stupeur: Tendence à la Demence. Traitement par l'extrait (principe Resineux de Cannabis Indica), Guerison', *Gazette des Hôpitaux Civils et Militaires*, vol. 30, 1857, p. 391.

MUNCH, J. C., 'Marihuana and Crime', *U.N. Bulletin on Narcotics*, vol. 18, no. 2, 1966, pp. 15–22.

MURPHY, H. B. M., 'The Cannabis Habit', *U.N. Bulletin on Narcotics*, vol. 15, no. 1, 1963, pp. 15–23.

NEWMARK, PETER, *Out of Your Mind?*, Penguin, 1968.

O'SHAUGHNESSY, W. B., 'On the Preparation of the Indian Hemp, or Gunjah', *Translations of the Medical and Physical Society of Calcutta*, vol. 8, no. 2, 1842, pp. 421–61.

PATERSON, ALAN, *Legal Aid as a Social Service*, Cobden Trust, 1970.

PATON, W. D. M., 'Drug Dependence – A Socio-Pharmacological Assessment', *Advancement of Science*, December 1968, pp. 200–212.

DE PINHO, R., *et al.*, 'Problemas Socio-Psicologicos de Macanhismo', *Neurobiologia*, vol. 25, 1962, pp. 9–19.

POROT, A., 'Le Cannabisme (Hashich, Kif, Chira, Marihuana)', *Annales Médico-Psychologiques*, vol. 100, no. 1, 1942, pp. 1–24.

REYNOLDS, J. R., 'On the Therapeutical Uses and Toxic Effects of Cannabis Indica', *Lancet*, vol. 1, 1890, pp. 637–8.

ROBB, JAMES, *Working Class Anti-Semite*, Tavistock, 1954.

ROSEVEAR, JOHN, *Pot: A Handbook of Marihuana*, University Books, New York, 1967.

SCHOFIELD, MICHAEL, *The Sociological Aspects of Homosexuality*, Longmans, 1965.

SCHOFIELD, MICHAEL, *The Sexual Behaviour of Young People*, Penguin, 1968.

SCHOFIELD, MICHAEL, *Social Research*, Heinemann, 1969.

SCOTT, P. D., and WILLCOX, D. R., 'Delinquency and the Amphetamines', *British Journal of Addiction*, vol. 61, November 1965, pp. 9–27.

SILBERMAN, MARTIN, *Aspects of Drug Addiction*, The Royal London Prisoners' Aid Society, 1967.

SOLOMON, DAVID, (Ed.), *The Marihuana Papers*, Panther, 1969.

TAYLOR, F., and REY, J. H., 'The Scapegoat Motif In Society and Its Manifestation in a Therapeutic Group', *International Journal of Psychoanalysis*, vol. 34, 1953, pp. 253–64.

TELLA, A., ASUNTI, T., TINUBO, K., and SESSI, J., 'Indian Hemp Smoking', *Journal of Social Health Nigeria*, January 1967, pp. 40–50.

TYLDEN, E., 'Cannabis Taking in England', *Newcastle Medical Journal*, vol. 30, no. 6, 1968.

WALTON, R. P., *Marijuana: America's New Drug Problem*, Lippincott, Philadelphia, 1938.

WATT, J. M., 'Drug Dependence of Hashish Type' In *Hashish: Its Chemistry and Pharmacology*, CIBA Foundation Study Group, 21, Churchill, 1965.

WEIL, A. T., ZINBERG, NORMAN, and NELSON, J. M., 'Clinical and Psychological Effects of Marijuana in Man', *Science*, vol. 162, 1968, p. 1234.

WESTWOOD, GORDON, *Society and the Homosexual*, Gollancz, 1952.

WESTWOOD, GORDON, *A Minority*, Longmans, 1960.

WOLFF, P. O., *Marihuana in Latin America: The Threat It Constitutes*, Linacre Press, Washington, 1949.

ZINBERG, NORMAN, and WEIL, A. T., 'Cannabis: The First Controlled Experiment', *New Society*, vol. 13, no. 329, 1969, pp. 84–6.

ZINBERG, NORMAN, and WEIL, A. T., 'A Comparison of Marihuana Users and Non-Users', *Nature*, vol. 226, 1970, p. 119.

Reports

The Indian Hemp Drugs Commission Report, 1893–4, Simla, 1897.

Mayor's Committee on Marihuana, New York, *The Marihuana Problem in the City of New York. Sociological, Medical, Psychological and Pharmacological Studies*, Cattell, Lancaster Pennsylvania, 1944.

Proceedings of the White House Conference on Narcotics and Drug Abuse, US Government Printing Office, Washington, 1962.

The President's Commission on Law Enforcement and Administration of Justice, *Task Force Report: Narcotics and Drug Abuse*, US Government Printing Office, Washington, 1967.

Ontario Addiction Research Foundation, *Addictions*, vol. 15, no. 1, 1968.

Drugs and Civil Liberties, National Council for Civil Liberties, 1969.

Report of the Advisory Committee on Drug Dependence, *Cannabis* (Wootton report), HMSO, 1969.

Report by the Advisory Committee on Drug Dependence, *Powers of Arrest and Search in Relation to Drug Offences* (Deedes report), HMSO, 1970.

Canadian Commission of Inquiry into the Non-Medical Use of Drugs (Le Dain Report), Ottawa, 1970.

Index of Names

Subject Index

More about Penguins and Pelicans

Penguinews, which appears every month, contains details of all the new books issued by Penguins as they are published. From time to time it is supplemented by *Penguins in Print*, which is a complete list of all books published by Penguins which are in print. (There are well over three thousand of these.)

A specimen copy of *Penguinews* will be sent to you free on request, and you can become a subscriber for the price of the postage. For a year's issues (including the complete lists) please send 30p if you live in the United Kingdom, or 60p if you live elsewhere. Just write to Dept EP, Penguin Books Ltd, Harmondsworth, Middlesex, enclosing a cheque or postal order, and your name will be added to the mailing list.

Another Pelican is described overleaf.

Note: *Penguinews* and *Penguins in Print* are not available in the U.S.A. or Canada

A Penguin Special

The Non-Medical Use of Drugs

Here is a direct, clearly written, and very human survey of
today's drug scene in all its aspects. The writers understand
'drug' to mean any sedative, stimulant, tranquillizing,
hallucinogenic, or other psychotropic chemical – a definition
that takes in alcohol and tobacco as well as more notorious
substances like marijuana, hashish, LSD, heroin and 'speed'.
Their report does much more than consider the drugs
themselves – it examines in eye-opening detail every
dimension of non-medical drug use and drug-related
behaviour, including the religious and the sexual. In addition
the book offers an in-depth view of one country's use of law
as a response to the drug explosion.

Undertaken by the Canadian government, the research on
which this book is based was never allowed to stray from the
actual experiences of people who use drugs. In fact coffee
houses and universities played a key role in the investigation.
And among the six appendices is a special section of letters
from private citizens – some warmly in favour of wider
legalization – others indignant in their expressions of grief and
outrage.

When this volume appeared in Canada it created a sensation.
Its recommendations, which are often surprising, will provoke
as much discussion in other countries. For drugs, whether they
bring delight to the senses or death to the body, are now a
phenomenon that no one can ignore.

NOT FOR SALE IN CANADA

Another Pelican by Michael Schofield
The Sexual Behaviour of Young People

NOT FOR SALE IN THE U.S.A.